Craig Hovey is Assistant ...
University, Ohio. He is the
ing, most recently, *Bearing* ...*,* *witness in Chris-*
tian Practice (Eerdmans, 2011) and *Nietzsche and Theology*
(T&T Clark, 2008). He also co-edited *An Eerdmans Reader in
Contemporary Political Theology* (Eerdmans, 2011). Dr. Hovey
holds a degree in biology from the University of California,
San Diego and a Ph.D. in Christian theology and ethics from
the University of Cambridge. He lives in Ashland, Ohio with
his wife and two sons.

WHAT MAKES US MORAL?

Science, religion, and the shaping
of the moral landscape:
A Christian response to Sam Harris

Craig Hovey

First published in Great Britain in 2012

Society for Promoting Christian Knowledge
36 Causton Street
London SW1P 4ST
www.spckpublishing.co.uk

British Library Cataloguing-in-Publication Data
A catalogue record for this book is available from the British Library

ISBN 978–0–281–06898–2
eBook ISBN 978–0–281–06899–9

Typeset by Caroline Waldron, Wirral, Cheshire
First printed in Great Britain by Ashford Colour Press
Subsequently digitally printed in Great Britain

eBook by Graphicraft Limited, Hong Kong

Produced on paper from sustainable forests

For William

Contents

To every human problem, there is a solution that is simple, neat, and wrong.

Walter Lippmann

Preface

———•◦•———

Is science really all we need? If we're not there yet, will reason and science someday soon be able to tell us everything we need to know about how to live a good life? Is religion becoming less and less important in our pursuit of life's deepest and most urgent questions?

In *The Moral Landscape*, popular atheist writer Sam Harris says yes.

He is wrong.

*

Before studying theology, I gained an enthusiasm for biology in my youth thanks to an extraordinarily gifted teacher. He was an atheist and I was a Christian. Both intent on evangelizing, we probably just annoyed each other. Perhaps at some level we were enemies. But he taught me to love science and I always knew he believed in my ability to excel at it.

The antagonisms we've been sold are often grievously overdrawn. This is especially true of the science and religion debate, which often strikes me as reductionistic and contrived. I resist much of that debate, preferring to keep alive ways of affirming a greater complexity to things. Life always surprises and, as a friend likes to say, "people are big places." As a Christian ethicist, I work to re-imagine life with the enemies we've been told we have. We'll certainly have enemies. But loving them, as Jesus taught, must involve more than refusing to kill them. As the theologian John Howard Yoder writes, "my adversary is part of my truth-finding process."[1]

This is how I think about the common supposition that science and religion are competing over the same turf. It's also how I hope to engage with enemies like Sam Harris. Even if "enemy" sounds a bit strong, it somehow keeps me looking for ways to move the conversation into deeper waters.

*

I would like to express my thanks to friends and colleagues who helped me look into these matters with more insight than would have been possible on my own: Jason Barnhart, my research assistant, and two of my outstanding students: Jake Ewing and Joe Antus. I am especially indebted to my colleague Pete Slade who, from an early stage, aided me in conceiving of the project as a whole. He also read the entire manuscript, offering his wise counsel. Any blunders that slipped through are mine, while many of the best points likely originated with Pete. This book is dedicated to my son William, who loves science and God.

Some of the material in Chapter 4 originally appeared in a different form in "Christian Ethics as Good News" in *Imaginative Apologetics: Theology, Philosophy and the Catholic Tradition*, ed. Andrew Davison (London: SCM Press, 2011).

Introduction

———◆———

My grandfather preached the gospel of Christ; my father preached the gospel of socialism; I preach the gospel of science.

Sir Richard Gregory (1864–1952)[1]

The 2009 comedy film *The Invention of Lying* is set in a world in which it's impossible to lie. But one day the lead character, played by Ricky Gervais, somehow does the impossible. Grieving at the bedside of his dying mother, he lies about what awaits her after death. It won't be an eternity of nothingness, he says, but a reunion with everyone she has ever loved. She will be young again, free of pain, and full of happiness and love. Viewers are struck by how normal this kind of consolation is. In the film, the mother dies happy. But in a world that knows only how to speak the truth, this is a happiness that comes from deception.

An avowed atheist with a university degree in philosophy, Gervais exposes how the deep human desire to be happy is very often at odds with a fierce honesty about the way things are. If the biggest lies are religious ones—such as those that speak of eternal blessedness—then billions of people would rather be happy than truthful. Sadly, this also means they can't really be happy either.

Gervais is a member of the advisory board for Sam Harris's non-profit organization, Project Reason. He and Harris are *morally* committed to rejecting all religious belief in the name of honesty and truth. Religion is based on lies, as Harris remarks:

Anyone who thinks he knows for sure that Jesus was born of a virgin or that the Qur'an is the perfect word of the Creator of the universe is lying. Either he is lying to himself, or to everyone else. In neither case should such false certainties be celebrated.[2]

The certainties afforded by science and reason are one thing; religious ones are quite another. In our world of competing religious certainties, Harris hopes to transcend them by commending a science of morality.

Harris belongs to a cadre of "New Atheists."[3] With Daniel Dennett, Richard Dawkins, and the late Christopher Hitchens, Harris speaks for a contemporary brand of atheism that, appealing to reason and science, goes on the offensive against religious belief of all kinds. These writers have been criticized for focusing much more on destroying their opponents military-style than on offering a constructive, atheistic alternative to them. In this respect, they differ markedly from their atheist companion from an earlier age, Friedrich Nietzsche (1844–1900).

Give me that old-time atheism

When Nietzsche saw nineteenth-century Europe moving away from Christianity, he also knew that people wanted to hold on to a basically Christian morality. In his fictional account *Thus Spoke Zarathustra*, a madman comes down from the hills in order to announce to the world that God is dead and "you have killed him!" The world would need to create a whole new morality. It couldn't simply keep the old one that depended on Christianity. Society must gird up its loins and boldly strike out into uncharted territory, inventing a new morality that has nothing to do with meekness and compassion. The new morality prizes strength rather than weakness, nobility rather than vulnerability.

Paradoxically, Nietzsche took Christian morality much more seriously than the New Atheism does. He understood that, despite the frequent failures of Christians to live up to it, Christianity celebrates compassion and costly generosity; it brings good news to the poor and weak, counsels loving enemies and welcoming foreigners, commands visiting prisoners, feeding the hungry, clothing the naked, caring for the ill, and being with the dying; it destroys barriers between ethnic groups and the genders; it prefers justice to seizing the handles of sovereign power; and it offers up every Christian believer to complete strangers in that utterly committed form of self-giving love: sacrifice.

Nietzsche knew that these things are what Christianity is all about—*and he hated it.* He thought nothing indicated resignation and defeat more than Jesus's teaching, "blessed are the meek." It's an ethic of and by losers, produced by resentment at seeing others who are strong, well off, and noble. You will know who the weak are by their desire for revenge against the strong. Resentment festers among them, infecting their character, and taking root so deeply that eventually a whole new set of values emerges—something very like the entire Sermon on the Mount. To Nietzsche, Christian morality poisons a resolute determination to embrace life at its most tragic. It's a "slave morality" that whines about the slightest injustice and elevates those whose single worth lies in a self-absorbed victim-mentality. These weaklings are apt to bleed to death from a scratch while the noble soul marches on, quickly scorning the past for its insignificance.[4]

The urgent human project, for Nietzsche, was to overthrow the old (Christian) morality preoccupied with compassion, meekness, forgiveness, and justice. An entirely new morality must emerge that thinks nothing of heaven—of eternal rewards, of petty gods and their wrath—but only of the earth. For this we would need a new culture and generation to build moral values that in every respect get us "back to the body, back to life, that it may give the earth a meaning, a human meaning." Nietzsche's fictional mouthpiece tries to rouse the crowds from their complacency: "Let your spirit and your virtue serve the sense of the earth, my brothers; and let the value of all things be posited newly by you. For that shall you be fighters! For that shall you be creators!"[5]

When it really counts, the New Atheism—which placed signs on London buses with the tepid message "There's probably no God. Now stop worrying and enjoy your life"—lacks Nietzsche's boldness. Its moral project is quite different from Nietzsche's. New Atheist writers like Sam Harris essentially want to hang on to what they consider to be the best of Christian morality. They only aspire to show that science and reason can get us to this morality much more quickly and consistently. It's true their disdain of religion is every bit as rhetorically overblown as their old-time unbelieving forebears'. But where they critique Christian morality, it's usually on the basis of a cavalier *dependence* on a genuinely benign moral sense that Nietzsche, for one, would have found profoundly embarrassing. Where have all the Nietzsches gone?

Nietzsche's moral program is much more ruthless than Harris's. Yet as a Christian I much prefer Nietzsche. To me, he exemplifies the advice of German theologian Dietrich Bonhoeffer (1906–45), who urged Christians to engage the unbelieving world at its strongest point, not its weakest. Nietzsche returns the favor. He went right to the core of Christianity in order to reject it. Christians really do celebrate the humility and weakness that Nietzsche so despised. He was right to see that dispensing with Christianity would require nothing less than a complete revolution in everything we value.

By comparison, Harris is disappointingly conventional on moral topics. There are no real revelations when it comes to the benevolence science and reason supposedly demand of us. But this is because he doesn't engage with Christianity at its strongest point—at its core morality. Without admitting it, he mostly adopts it. He is then content to expose Christianity's weakest points and declare small victories. In Harris's hands, all religions are reduced to "religion," all religion to "faith," and all faith to unfounded certainty.[6] Christianity is robbed of its genuine moral distinctives, which Harris either doesn't know or doesn't care about. I wrote this book because Christian morality cannot be shown the door quite so easily.

Beware of "obvious"

Reading and re-reading Harris's book *The Moral Landscape*, I became convinced that there is a single, fundamental error that time and again can be seen underlying many of the book's flawed arguments.

Very often Harris points out what is "clearly" the case and shows what is so "obvious" that no further argument is needed. In nearly every instance, Harris simplifies complex matters and expresses impatience with anyone who insists that things are more complicated. To him, suicide bombers are *only* motivated by afterlife rewards. Muslims are *obviously* irrational in their response to cartoons depicting Muhammad. Catholics are *clearly* deluded in opposing condom distribution in sub-Saharan Africa. With some reluctance, I came to see that Harris has a childlike urge to make matters easier than they are and to drown out what others are saying rather than contend with them with patience and care. It's true, not everything people believe is right. But I came to be suspicious of a strategy that appeals to what is "obvious" and I resolved to try and notice what's being overlooked.

Here's an example of what I mean. *The Moral Landscape* ends on an optimistic note. While acknowledging that racism is still a problem in American society, Harris nevertheless observes that moral progress in this and other areas is "unmistakable." We are "clearly" becoming more empathetic and today we can "surely" expect to act with the good of all humanity in mind more so than we ever have before.[7] And yet scholars challenge such confidence, especially when it comes to race in America.

They note that if we see racism as a constant across time (as opposed to a variable), we will be misled, measuring today's racism according to the standards that were in place at the time of slavery. Concluding that racism is steadily declining, we might convince ourselves that our societies are even displaying the moral progress that Harris claims for them. But the best sociology on the subject says it isn't so.[8] Too strong a determination to congratulate one's own culture results in blindness to how forms of racism and race-relations change over time.

In the following chapters, the main case I make against Harris is along these lines. In his *New York Times* review of *The Moral Landscape*, Kwame Anthony Appiah objects that

> the landscape that the book calls to mind is that of a city a few days after a snowstorm. A marvelously clear avenue stretches before us, but the looming banks to either side betray how much has been unceremoniously swept aside.[9]

In the name of simple, clear, and obvious reason—reason rooted in our humanity as such rather than culture—quite a lot falls through the cracks. Modern, universal knowledge of the sort Harris seeks produces collateral damage precisely in the places where it is busily applauding its own morality and evenhandedness.

As a result, the Christian responses most appropriate to the work of Sam Harris are far deeper and more fundamental than offering up piecemeal rebuttals to his critiques. There is much more at stake. What is going to become of those things that have been swept aside? In the end, can we entertain a vision of the good life and human flourishing that neither simplifies complex questions in the name of rationality nor generates victims never seen and heard in the name of what is moral?

What this book is and isn't

I wrote this book with Christians in mind. I certainly hope that any reader will find something worthwhile within these pages. But I won't pretend that all comers will be equally satisfied by how I argue my case. There's a long history of Christians defending the faith, especially against misunderstanding. Early Christian apologists defended against accusations that they were teaching atheism (for refusing to worship the Roman deities) and cannibalism (for eating and drinking Jesus Christ's body and blood). Later apologists in dialogue with Islam defended the doctrine of the Trinity against being misunderstood as a teaching about three gods.

While this book can be seen as continuing the Christian apologetic tradition in being mostly negative—showing where and why Harris is mistaken about morality—this is because of what I want to defend. Readers who don't think Christian morality is worth defending may not see the point. They will almost certainly fail to make much sense of the final chapter in which I set out Christianity's better alternative.

Christians sometimes defend their theological convictions by insulating them from scientific questioning. One common Christian defense goes like this: science restricts itself to what is the case and the nature of the universe; whereas theology asks questions like "Why is there something rather than nothing?" Harris represents a style of doing science (sometimes called "scientism" by critics) that boldly and self-consciously oversteps these traditional boundaries. Crossing from science to ethics is the central move in his recent work. He moves from *describing* (science) to *prescribing* (ethics). Even though there are significant problems with doing this, I believe it is a mistake to mount an all-out defense of these boundaries. Here's why.

In Terry Eagleton's inimitable critique of the New Atheists, *Reason, Faith, and Revolution: Reflections on the God Debate*, he upholds a version of these boundaries:

The difference between science and theology, as I understand it, is one over whether you see the world as a gift or not; and you cannot resolve this just by inspecting the thing, any more than you can deduce from examining a porcelain vase that it is a wedding present.[10]

I disagree with Eagleton somewhat. Simply observing something—whether the universe or a porcelain vase—often tells us nothing about what is most significant about it. Then again, many people agree that a porcelain vase might make a very nice wedding present in a way that a bag of yesterday's garbage wouldn't. Our ideas about friendship, love, gift-giving, weddings, and home decor lead us to think this way. It's *plausible* that the vase was a gift. "Simply" looking at it is never simple, since we see things with a certain aesthetic eye. Seeing comes from aesthetic beliefs, formation, and judgments that we learn over time by being members of a certain culture and so forth. In the same way, "whether you see the world as a gift or not" is not *entirely* separate from "just inspecting the thing." It's just that our inspecting and our seeing turn out to be more complicated than merely opening our eyes.

The philosopher Ludwig Wittgenstein (1889–1951) asks us to imagine trying to convince someone else that a blossoming flower is marvelous and beautiful. If they just don't appreciate it, try as you may, pretty soon all you will be left with is the appeal: "Just look at it opening out!"[11] This means no one can know for certain that a blossoming flower is marvelous just by looking at it. Then again, many of us would say that failing to "see" such beauty is failing to see something that, in some sense, *really is* the most important thing about flowers.

I'm interested in the meaning of the phrase "in some sense" here. In what sense? Surely some aesthetic sense. But also in a sense that we might want to say is objective but also frustratingly beyond one's ability to convince those who just don't see it.

I don't try in this book to convince those who don't see it. I won't try to prove the existence of God. Nor will I attempt by dint of sheer reason to promote a more distinctively Christian account of morality than Harris gives. This is no modesty on my part, though I confess to having doubts about *all* purely rational moral accounts (since I doubt that we are ever fully in possession of reason alone). Rather, just as I am at one with orthodox Christianity when it teaches about a God who embraces material existence in order to disclose the true meaning of the material, I also believe that the most satisfying moral landscape is one that exceeds our abilities to create it.

What would it be then? It would be more gospel than law, more about good news and permission than prohibition and limitation. But it would also cost us something. If it's not our own creation, we would be more likely to bind ourselves to it (would we really stick with a morality that we made up?). It would appeal to our aesthetic sense and more closely resemble art than science. Maybe the most appropriate thing to say about it is ultimately "Just look at it opening out!"

*

A few mundane matters. I don't argue that only Christians can be "good people." Many people of other faiths, as well as those of no faith, are good in nearly all senses of the word. Many Christians are not. Nor do I claim that bad Christians aren't real Christians. Most "real" Christians know how to say both "Forgive me, Father, for I have sinned" and "I believe; help my unbelief" (Mark 9.24). But I do argue for Christianity's distinctive account of goodness and happiness.

Harris ruthlessly skewers hypocrites and know-it-all religious fundamentalists as well as wimpy liberals who cower from taking a stand on anything at all. Where Christians warrant a firm berating, we could not hope for more willing assistance than Harris provides. In my view, much of it is well-deserved; often I am even grateful for it.

Most of Harris's writings are animated by a moral sense on concrete matters that readers should approve of (in fact he counts on it). Whether the issue is homelessness, violence against women, or lying, he is a passionate advocate for what many people would call a straightforwardly rigorous ethic that places a high premium on the well-being of humans and animals. This is not all there is, but it is commendable.

As a fellow writer, I admire Harris's commitment to arguing his thesis while minimizing the use of philosophical jargon. I try to do the same.

Finally, I have found no way to head off all criticisms like "But at a conference Harris said such and such" or "You've missed his reply to this certain blog post." The reason is that *Sam Harris is a full-time job.* He tirelessly defends his positions in person and in writing, fully utilizing the internet and other media. In addition to Harris's own website (samharris. org), one finds scores of YouTube clips, blogs, and debates. His career seems to be built on saying something provocative or outrageous in print and then spending the next few years defending himself in more measured ways. Even though it's unsportsmanlike of him, I've tried to keep up as best I can.

1

The gospel according to Sam Harris

———•◆•———

If there were a way for you and those you care about to be much
happier than you now are, would you want to know about it?

Sam Harris, *The Moral Landscape*[1]

[Winston] knew in advance what O'Brien would say [...]. That the
choice for mankind lay between freedom and happiness, and that,
for the great bulk of mankind, happiness was better.

George Orwell, *1984*

Sam Harris is an evangelist. He bears a gospel message about
increasing happiness, mitigating human suffering, and promoting personal and collective well-being. To anyone uninterested in this good news, he replies with the enthusiasm of a
new convert: Why wouldn't you want to be happy?

In *The Moral Landscape*, Harris unfolds the following argument. Moral questions only make sense when they involve conscious creatures (there is no morality about rocks, for instance).
Consciousness matters because only conscious creatures
can experience happiness and suffering. Furthermore, consciousness has to do with wholly natural phenomena experienced by our brains. Because science can study the brains of
conscious creatures, it can tell us what promotes happiness and
suffering. Therefore, moral questions have objectively right
and wrong answers that science can provide. We shouldn't
take people at their word when they claim to know what is
moral and what advances happiness. They might be wrong or

deluded. Equipped with the findings of science, enlightened people and cultures can speak with confidence about moral rightness and stop respecting the views of people and cultures that are simply wrong.

From this short summary, it's easy to recognize the two groups with which Harris most disagrees. He identifies them as believers in religion and cultural relativism. "Religious" people believe things on faith rather than reason and so already think they know answers that only science can provide.[2] It is no surprise that different religions have differing ideas about what life is for, what makes us happy, and how we ought to act. In a world where different groups disagree on fundamental questions like these, there is bound to be conflict. And if we lack the ability to rise above the parochial answers that religions provide—if we are unable to arrive at a universal morality that applies to everyone regardless of their particular beliefs—there is no end in sight for these struggles. They will go on interminably, which obviously threatens any straightforward ideas about human happiness.

Cultural relativists allow the conflict and disagreement to persist. Harris has no patience with this mostly secular doctrine. In their attempt to understand the morality of other people and cultures on their own terms, relativists disable their ability to declare the wrongness of these others. Harris brings up cultural practices like Muslim women wearing burqas and female genital mutilation that, in the name of a sentimental respect for cultural differences, many Western intellectuals are reluctant to condemn. The "noble savage" is immune from critique. But if moral questions have objectively right and wrong answers, as Harris argues, there is no reason to be shy about reproving those ideas and practices that are objectively wrong. In fact, it would be wrong to shrink from reprimanding them.

Harris's thesis depends on at least three crucial ideas, all of which I address in this and later chapters. The first is that science and reason are grouped together and prized for their universality and objectivity. Neither is taken to be culturally, socially, or historically determined. The findings of science and the operations of reason are timeless as well as unconnected to prevailing variables like political concerns and economic conditions. This makes them superior to other attempts, including religious ones, to weigh in on moral questions. The second idea is that all religions, despite their differences, are essentially the same when it comes to how they conceive of the good life. They rely on faith—here taken by Harris to be the polar opposite of science—which involves holding beliefs without sufficient evidence. Third is the idea that cultural relativism, in assiduously trying to understand different societies, dismisses moral questions from consideration. Harris believes this moral reluctance threatens to contaminate all sciences with undue sensitivity to religious and other beliefs. As he says, "In the spirit of religious tolerance, most scientists are keeping silent when they should be blasting the hideous fantasies of a prior age with all the facts at their disposal."[3]

Seeing things this way means accepting that science and religion are in utter and irreconcilable contradiction. Harris claims that "religion and science are in a zero-sum conflict with respect to facts."[4] In 2006, Harris took part in an interdisciplinary forum called The Edge devoted to the forum's annual question, "What is your dangerous idea?" His answer ran under the threatening title, "Science Must Destroy Religion." He made clear that there is no way for science and religion to coexist. "The success of science often comes at the expense of religious dogma; the maintenance of religious dogma always comes at the expense of science."[5]

With clearly defined enemies and a willingness to make threats in the name of science, where is all of this headed? At first, Harris appears only to be interested in making the world more livable and peaceful, a world in which science reigns. But beneath what he believes to be a consummately balanced and reasonable vision lies a brave new world.

Consider: What should we do with deluded people? What about whole cultures that have false beliefs about human happiness? Perhaps they believe in God—that God is good and we ought to be too. Perhaps they place hope in eternity, deferring happiness in this life. Perhaps they have other irrational fears or superstitions, or mistaken beliefs that drive them to separate men from women at mealtimes or cause them to sacrifice children in order to ensure a good harvest. What ought *we* do with *them*?

When answering these questions, it matters greatly who the "we" is. It is unmistakable that Harris has in mind the advanced scientific cultures of the West. This "we" has experienced a renaissance in its understanding of reason as part of its history. "We" have long held power—academic, military, political—so that questions about what *we* should do with *them* are not simply theoretical. "We" really are in a position to do something powerful when it comes to the irrationality and immorality of others. We can realistically intervene and try to stop them. It goes without saying that this "we" includes Harris himself and those who think like he does.

Harris has a habit of framing complex matters in extremely stark terms like us-versus-them. It is a habit bequeathed to Harris by his particular intellectual and political culture. An example will help to make this point clearer. Christine Walley, an anthropologist at MIT who has studied female genital mutilation in African societies, as well as among immigrants to Western countries, notes that ever since Westerners began discussing this topic in the 1990s, they have generally adopted an all-or-nothing approach of "moral opprobrium or relativistic tolerance." She goes on to argue that "[t]his commonality is a hardened view of 'culture' based on a rigid essentialist notion of difference that can be historically linked to the colonial era."[6] Her analysis tries to understand the reasons why issues like this one have become so widely discussed.

I intend to draw attention to the responsibility that Westerners hold for the terms of these debates—interest in Europe and the United States stems not only from feminist or humanist concern, but also from the desire to sensationalize, to titillate, and to call attention to differences between "us" and "them" in ways that reaffirm notions of Western cultural superiority.[7]

Walley is trying to overcome the rigid us–them division on which so many other binaries are built. Then again, Harris despises anthropology. Perhaps this is why.

If there is something imperial about this clear-cut antagonism between us and them, it is helpful to understand the recent political context that surrounds everything Harris writes. Harris's ideas are the product of a deeply contemporary anxiety and cultural insecurity. Writing soon after the terrorist attacks of September 11, 2001, Harris adopted wholesale the most politically charged ways of framing them at that time. In this view, the West was engaged in a clash of civilizations with the Muslim world; America was at war with Islam itself; the starkness of civilized versus uncivilized, enlightened versus superstitious, was undeniable.

Demand for an objective and universal reason in order to rise above it all is an understandable impulse in dark times. The West has been here before. The acclaimed philosopher Stephen Toulmin has shown that similar anxieties birthed the intellectual projects of modernity.[8] He discusses René Descartes, arguably the first truly modern philosopher, who claimed that we can be certain of what we know in just the same way that we are certain that a triangle has three sides. Toulmin demonstrates that this emerging optimism, that reason could be as reliable and indisputable as geometry, makes sense in light of specific political uncertainties in early seventeenth-century France. Compared to humanist thinkers in the previous century, Descartes's confidence in reason alone placed enormous stock in theory, formal systems of logic, and demonstrable certainty while downplaying experience, tradition, and a "reasonable" modesty about one's own capacities and judgments. Descartes was optimistic about the world reason would create.

A brave new world

It is widely accepted that the First World War put an end to this optimism. Such vast destruction took the steam out of any form of confident belief in history's sure and steady progress. As the twentieth century unfolded, it became less and less possible to hold on to any such notions. The overconfident optimism of the movement Descartes helped set in motion was forced to tip its hand. Throughout what ought to have been the playing fields of the world's most enlightened peoples were strewn battlefields of carnage and devastation.

Many reacted to the terrorist attacks of 9/11 in the same way. If there was a kind of post-cold war, secular, globalized utopia, 9/11 showed it to be a delusion. Religion and all manner of "unreason" are in fact still important. If there was a brave new world on its way, the supposed backwardness of religious belief still spoils it, just as it has done during several hundred years of attempting to surpass it.

Whether we point to the Great War or to 9/11, it is a mistake to lash out as though the project of reason hadn't been given enough of a chance and, like the twin towers, had been brought crashing down by enemies of reason. This is a self-serving but false tale. A great deal of violence had been hidden in the name of being unnecessary in an age that supposedly had learned to overcome conflict with reason. But the violence was now exposed as a very real entailment in bringing about the uniformity that many assumed was being realized by other means. "Reason" of this sort only *pretends* to want peace; it harbors real violence. (I grew up in California in the 1980s, an era sometimes thought of as progressive and economically expansive. I now recall my dismay at later learning how President Reagan's many wars in the Americas and elsewhere made such thinking possible.) This association between violence and reason (at least, reason, as Harris conceives of it), is evident when Harris discusses happiness and global well-being.

Without a doubt, some people do not want what is really best for themselves and others. Your uncle may want a clean set of lungs, but may want to sustain a two-pack-a-day cigarette habit even more. We might all be happier if we desired differently, if we brought our desires more fully into accordance with the facts about ourselves and our world. What if someone did this *for us*? What if they did it without our consent, but knowing that we would be happier in the end? In a *Huffington Post* response to his critics, Harris asks readers to consider this very question.

We are to imagine a utopian world in which almost everyone "miraculously" acts in ways that lead to the most happiness for themselves and others. It would be an "earthly paradise." But there are a few dissenters: a few are psychopaths, some others are determined to commit acts of violence. In order to make these renegades get with the happiness program, science offers the solution of painlessly changing what they value. After a "firmware update," everyone without exception now desires the well-being of all. "Now the entirety of the species is fit to live in a global civilization that is as safe, and as fun, and as interesting, and as filled with love as it can be." The dissenters now realize the happiness they were missing before.[9]

I confess to finding this scenario horrifying. It is presented as a defense of the idea that happiness and well-being are objective realities about which people can be gravely deluded. The good news of Harris's gospel message is that happiness is possible. No amount of re-education programs and brainwashing can tarnish the paradisal vision of a happy society because, by definition, it is a society that couldn't be better. Elsewhere Harris expresses his hope that neuroimaging will someday soon improve our world through better lie detection.

Wouldn't we all be better off if, when the truth really matters, "it became impossible to lie"? And "wherever important conversations are held, the truthfulness of all participants will be monitored."[10] By the way, he acknowledges that there is a long legal tradition against forcing people to testify. But he considers this to be "a relic of a more superstitious age" when people believed they would face eternity in hell if they were to lie under oath rather than keep silent. So forcing people to testify is also part of Harris's image of a better world. But let us ask whether it really would be better.

The question is whether a world in which some people are reprogramed by force in order to desire the right things is better ("as filled with love as it can be") than a world in which people are free to make hells by following their diseased desires. It may be impossible to imagine a perfectly happy world without love. But is it truly love without the unhappy possibility that it will go unmet? Loving opens us up to tragedy and sorrow that, if ruled out, would probably alter love itself beyond all recognition. Doesn't this leave us with only a sterile vision? What would we miss out on if it became impossible to tell lies in certain situations? While Harris knows his "miraculous" scenario will never happen (although he says we are close to having the lie detectors he describes), it doesn't stop him from experimenting with some quasi-religious mumbo jumbo.

In Harris's utopian scenario, science is omniscient savior. Scientists know what is best for everyone and confidently act as thought-police, administering the necessary fixes to human brains as they see fit. It should go without saying that in the real world, science has actually done this. The examples are numerous. Between 1929 and 1974, for example, the state of North Carolina sterilized 7,528 of its citizens who were criminals or mentally ill. Overseeing the sterilizations was the state Eugenics Board, which included members of the ominously named Institution for the Feeble-Minded. These undesirable members of the population may have *thought* they desired to reproduce. They may have imagined that doing so would bring happiness. According to some of the best science of the day, they were sorely mistaken.

The cost paid for reason's claim to be universal is often violence against those marked as irrational. Now, Harris dismisses attempts like this to show that his vision is not too distant from notorious horrors undertaken by science. He asks, "Is it really so difficult to distinguish between a science of morality and the morality of science?"[11] At least in practice, the answer appears to be *yes*—it is difficult. Science is not as objective as some believe. It produces victims. Those who trust in science and reason alone are likely to mimic forms of oppression and violence motivated by certainties very similar to the religious certainties they disdain.

Champion of empire

Other characteristics of Harris's landscape are just as frightening. The celebrated literary critic Terry Eagleton refers to some members of the New Atheism as the "intellectual wing of the war on terror."[12] The reason is that these writers supported recent justifications for the invasions of Afghanistan and Iraq, particularly on ideological grounds.[13] The dangers of radical Islam are seen as mere symptoms of a greater and more fundamental confrontation. The modern civilized world was waging war against "terror," a tactic that arises out of a religious ideology that refuses the secular lessons learned in the West. Violence waged in the name of nations and the ideas that birth them (freedom, liberty) is considered noble, but violence in the name of God is thought to be morally retrograde. One is reasonable; the other is irrational.

We have already seen how Harris's crusade sometimes slips into imitating the very irrationality he opposes. In his first book, *The End of Faith*, he argues at length that, however distasteful it may seem, torture is not morally different from causing the deaths of innocent civilians in war. In the ethics of war, noncombatant deaths are often justified as collateral damage. If the West is to engage in an all-out fight with the dangerous superstitions of Islam, then Harris counsels that torture may be "not only permissible but necessary."[14] We are to imagine the famous "ticking bomb" scenario in which a terrorist withholds vital information about the location of an imminent, deadly explosion somewhere in the city. If torture presents the best hope for discovering the location and saving hundreds of lives, it may be morally required.

Harris's argument is that the dictates of reason reveal that whatever intuitions we may have about torture's moral perversity, we must not be fooled by appearances. Harris assures readers that in the same way that a full moon on the horizon only looks bigger than when it is overhead, the feeling of unease over the question of torture is only an illusion "every bit as neurological as those that give rise to the moon illusion" (what this means is anyone's guess).[15]

The goal is to use rational argument in order to overcome what are really just illusions, feelings, appearances, and qualms. Comparing torture to collateral damage in war, Harris writes, "We cannot let our qualms over collateral damage paralyze us because our enemies know no such qualms."[16] What should we make of these qualms? Is Harris saying you are free to abandon your moral commitments if they are not shared or when it looks like they will get you into trouble? It seems so. And does Harris arrive at this conclusion by the pure light of reason? Is it delivered up through the empirical facts of science? This is doubtful. I will have much to say about qualms in a moment.

For now, let it be said that students of the venerable Just War tradition will immediately protest Harris's argument in favor of torture. The constraints governing entrance into war, as well as governing conduct while fighting, do not depend on the morality of the enemy. The principles of Just War are binding irrespective of whether enemy soldiers follow them. The tradition maintains an absolute prohibition against *intentionally* targeting civilians. Things are somewhat different when it comes to collateral damage, when civilians are *unintentionally* killed, including cases where their deaths are foreseen.

Harris is wrong to compare collateral damage to torture. Defending his position on his blog, he writes,

> Most assume my analogy fails in the following way: torture is the intentional infliction of guaranteed suffering, while collateral damage is the unintentional imposition of possible suffering (or death). Apples and oranges. But this isn't true. We often drop bombs knowing that innocent people will be killed or horribly injured by them.[17]

Yet Harris confuses *intending* with *knowing*, a difference described in ethics by the principle of Double Effect. An action may have two effects: bombing a military base may cause both the destruction of the base and the school next to it. Double Effect says that it may be justified to do it, *knowing* that the school will be destroyed as long as you did not *intend* to destroy the school. Some scholars dispute the legitimacy of Double Effect, but Harris shows no awareness of it. At the least, torture and collateral damage do in fact differ in respect of intention, regardless of whether one accepts Double Effect. It is only by ignoring the importance of intention that Harris can claim to have "successfully argued for the use of torture in any circumstance in which we would be willing to cause collateral damage."[18]

Still, one might ask, who cares about intention? Actually, Harris makes use of it when he wants to distinguish between the innocent dead of George Bush and those of terrorists. Knowing what is intended is what allows the killing of civilians to be classified as "collateral damage" in the first place. (It is also the only thing that lets you know whether cutting off a person's leg is surgical or sadistic.) But then why abandon the notion of intention when discussing torture? One cannot claim to torture someone unintentionally. As I will repeatedly point out in these pages, the important thing to notice is what has been excluded.

In this case, Harris has excluded what many people consider their natural, moral distaste for torture. With the help of cold logic, Harris thinks he can overcome what may be a deep-seated emotional antipathy for intentionally causing the suffering and pain of another human being. Even though his reasoning is faulty in ways I have been describing, he does not doubt that reason will help us keep our irrational prejudices in check.

But what would lead someone to think that what we might call our "pre-reflective" moral sense has *nothing* to do with morality? Suppose that when we bristle at the thought of torture, this is morally praiseworthy, even though it may not be something that is easy to understand rationally. We would only think we need to suppress the pre-reflective moral sense if we came to believe that reason is superior to it. We would be ranking cold reason above a moral sense that is perhaps the product of culture or of nature, or of both. Of course, Harris's entire project aims for us to rank things in this way. But it is something to argue for rather than assume. In other words, the success of Harris's main argument depends on having already accepted it! This is not very promising.

It gets worse. It turns out that the key element in Harris's gospel—increasing happiness, easing suffering—is not something Harris is prepared to show that we ought to value. Not, that is, based on reason and scientific evidence. His strategy is to assume that his readers already share these values. Perhaps they do. If so, the rest of the argument may go down easily (since there is not much left to argue). And since there is no inquiry into the source of this moral sense, it can be enlisted when convenient, just as it can also be abandoned at will.

Consider another example. In Chapter 2 of *The Moral Landscape*, Harris condemns the moral life of the Dobu islanders. He cites the distinguished anthropologist Ruth Benedict (1887–1948), who described the competitive Dobu culture as one of cruelty, superstition, and distrust. Their social life revolves around sorcery; good and bad events are thought to be tied to the sorcery practiced by one's neighbors. Moral judgment against them comes quickly and easily to Harris. "Once we more fully understand the neurophysiology of states like love, compassion, and trust, it will be possible to spell out the differences between ourselves and people like the Dobu in greater detail." But, he says, there's no need to wait on neuroscience to see that the Dobu are wrong when it comes to maximizing personal and social well-being.[19] Harris knows his readers, referring to "ourselves" as people to whom it is obvious that the Dobu are morally perverse. We don't believe in sorcery, so obviously it is foolish to structure a society around it. However, there is no argument here, only an appeal to *consensus* with like-minded readers. Earlier he dismissed consensus, claiming that it "in no way constrains what may or may not be true." For this we need science and reason.[20]

Why is Harris so inconsistent? Sometimes he relies on an assumed consensus shared by his readers while other times he feels the need to argue against it on supposedly purely rational grounds. This is precisely the point I am making about torture: what are we to make of Harris's marked disregard of our moral distaste for it? He confesses that "[M]any readers have found my views deeply unsettling. (For what it's worth, I do too. It would be much easier to simply be 'against torture' across the board and end the discussion.)"[21] Isn't there something eerily inhuman about this? Must we really be slaves to reason in this way? Are our moral intuitions so utterly unschooled, unreliable, and irrational that we must, on occasion, work at cross-purposes with them?

I am not claiming we should in every way trust our inclinations or refuse to reflect on why we happen to find some things morally repulsive. But there would be something odd and even terrifying about according them no moral significance in cases like torture, while granting them exclusive significance in cases like the Dobu's sorcery—precisely the point where one would expect Harris to subordinate them entirely to scientific reason.

I will cite just one more example of the inconsistency I'm talking about. Harris brings up research suggesting that conservatives are more likely than liberals to experience feelings of disgust, which may especially shape their moral attitudes on sexual matters.[22] It seems clear that Harris thinks that disgust should be overcome through the right use of reason. But he elsewhere relies on generating feelings of disgust in readers such as when he cites a psychopathic rapist's lengthy self-report.[23] Sometimes the objection "That's disgusting!" seems to warrant a response like "Get over it." While at other times Harris's response is "Yes, so see how wrong it is?"

In his searching review of Harris's book, Thomas Nagel, a philosopher at New York University, asks what he considers to be the key question: "Once we recognize the ways in which we have been formed by forces beyond our control, what resource can we nevertheless call on within ourselves in deciding *which of our instincts to transcend*?" Answering it, Nagel laments, is something for which Harris seems to have no patience.[24]

Who is the enemy?

Harris is obsessed with Islam, Islamic radicalism, terrorism, suicide bombers, and martyrdom. His writings are as much suffused with post-9/11 nervousness and outrage as with a measured determination to subject reality to reason alone. Reviewers frequently point out Harris's lack of subtlety especially concerning Islam, as though he thinks his outspokenness alone qualifies him to speak on the topic.[25]

Consider recent blog entries in which Harris recommends specifically profiling Muslims at airport security screenings. "We should profile Muslims, or anyone who looks like he or she could conceivably be Muslim, and we should be honest about it."[26] He admits to being baffled by comments that call his perspective racist and appalling, claiming that political correctness prevents us from being honest about the connection between suicidal terrorism and Islam. But what does it mean for someone to "look like he or she could conceivably be Muslim"? One person has responded to the idea that there is an easily identifiable "Muslim look" by creating a website called "Pictures of Muslims Wearing Things."[27] The reality is more complicated than Harris acknowledges.

One also notices the conveniently simple rubric Harris uses for understanding suicide terrorism. Why did the 9/11 hijackers commit their crimes? "Because they believed that they would go straight to paradise for doing so. It is rare to find the behavior of human beings so fully and satisfactorily explained. Why have we been reluctant to accept this explanation?"[28] He doesn't believe Western politicians when they claim that Islam is not the enemy, nor when they insist that Islam is a religion of peace. When it comes to terrorism, Harris dismisses the political factors on grounds that even though there are vast numbers of oppressed peoples, not all of them are driven to commit violent acts. No, he says, the matter is uncomplicated: Islam offers all the explanation needed. "Either you believe in martyrdom as a genuine metaphysical principle or you don't."[29] Singling out the religious aspect to suicide terrorism, on Harris's grounds, is a move that consigns it to unreason. These are not only acts that ought to be condemned for being immoral. They are proof positive of the irrationality of religion.

This is a typical Harris strategy. A complex matter is reduced to a single factor that will strike many readers as obviously silly or wrong-headed and therefore in no need of argument. It is a tacit appeal to consensus. Anyone who then wishes to mount a counter-argument is immediately identified as irrational, again without argument. It is an efficient strategy, even if it is intellectually grossly irresponsible.

Talal Asad, renowned anthropologist at the City University of New York, offers a much more nuanced analysis of suicide terrorism. He does not neglect the religious vocabulary used to describe it, but neither does he neglect to consider the political context out of which it arises. For example, is it conceivable that there would even be such a thing as a Palestinian suicide bomber if Palestine were a sovereign independent nation? Asad notes that popular support for Islamist movements dropped significantly immediately following the Oslo Accords in 1993. But when it became evident to many that Oslo would not have the political payoff it promised, support for these movements again rose in opinion polls.[30]

Similarly, Robert Pape at the University of Chicago, who studies suicide terrorism and is one of the most respected experts on the subject, argues for the centrality of the political factors.

> The data show that there is little connection between suicide terrorism and Islamic fundamentalism, or any one of the world's religions. [. . .] Rather, what nearly all suicide terrorist attacks have in common is a specific secular and strategic goal: to compel modern democracies to withdraw military forces from territory that the terrorists consider to be their homeland.[31]

According to Asad and many other scholars, the complex phenomenon of suicide terrorism cannot be reduced to a single factor like a belief in being rewarded after death with seventy-two virgins (as Harris claims). Reductionism of this kind serves the interests of a cultural hegemony and imperial power. As long as those in the West focus exclusively on religious motivations for terrorism, we can have clear consciences about the foreign exploits of our nations' militaries and businesses. The United States and Israel are free to think of themselves as civilizing, rational forces in the face of barbarity and irrationality.

Addressing this very tendency to identify suicide bombing as "religious terrorism," Asad notes that this "defines the bomber as morally underdeveloped—and therefore premodern—when compared with peoples whose civilized status is partly indicated by their secular politics and their private religion and whose violence is therefore in principle disciplined, reasonable, and just."[32] These are strong words. But I contend that they apply to Harris in their entirety.

When all is said and done, Harris's cozy relationship with empire is not limited to this obvious support for the Dick Cheneys of the world. His brave new world gives license to a new version of the old cultural superiorities. (Why try to understand why some women actually choose to wear a burqa?[33]) The end of faith need not mean the end of empire. Now civilization itself must be bravely defended by gallant rationalists. Whereas conquerors used to (and still do) color their imperialism with heartening beatific promises and reassuring divine mandates, the new imperialism dispenses with it. Harris promotes a swaggering confidence in telling other people that they are wrong and are not reasoning correctly. The next step is just as predicable as the history has shown: "We" must win or else reason itself is doomed. Wage war against unreason; torture when necessary.

Science and reason

For Harris, "reason" has less to do with employing deductive logic or syllogistic proofs and more to do with demanding that we only ever believe something when there is empirical evidence for it. This is why Harris wants to ground his moral program in "facts about the world." It would be irrational to believe anything that does not flow from such facts.

The first thing to notice about this approach is that reason here functions as an ideology. Harris wants it both ways. He wants to tie together facts and values through the use of reason. But those entitled to speak most competently and authoritatively about values turn out to be scientists (although only the brave new scientists), precisely because they can most claim to be *value-free* in their judgments. Which is it going to be? According to philosopher Slavoj Žižek, the reason this is ideology is that "it imitates the form of natural sciences without really being one."[34]

The trouble is that reason cannot authenticate itself. When a critic asks why reason is to be trusted, Harris can only point to why doing so is reasonable. It is circular, of course. But it is only pernicious and less than honest when one refuses to acknowledge this circularity. In truth, we can never entirely step outside of our modes of thinking and being in the world, including our cultures and languages, in order to measure them against some absolute standard. We really stand in the middle of the things we use (like reason and language), even when discussing those things.

Now, I admit there is something quite silly about some Christians saying that they believe the Bible because of some claim *within the Bible itself.* But even this can be seen as an honest admission of the middle character of how we know things. At their best, appeals to the Bible of this sort are shorthand for saying, "I stand within the tradition that thinks of itself in relation to the God of the Bible, understanding that that tradition partly speaks through the testimonies to this God, testimonies that Christians preserved and safeguarded by calling them Scripture." On its own, this is not a *proof* that the Bible is true. But neither, I would argue, is it irrational. It honestly attests to the fact that being in the middle of a tradition of knowing is not necessarily enhanced by trying to escape it.

Alister McGrath, a well-known Christian critic of the New Atheism, asks a question that numerous disciplines, including the philosophy of science, have long answered in the affirmative. "Might reason be shaped by hidden social and subconscious impulses so that what we believe to be pure reason is actually socially constructed and manipulated by our past history and subconscious motivations?"[35] This way of putting the question owes a lot to Karl Marx (1818–1883) and Sigmund

Freud (1856–1939), but it also accurately reflects a general suspicion that became especially evident in the nineteenth century—that *no* ideas transcend history and society. In some respects, Harris adopts this suspicion when it comes to his objections to moral relativism. It is obvious to him that culture and religion determine the differing moral values that millions of people hold. But these determinants are deemed wholly inadequate for a world come of age, a world that needs to dispense with so much mythology and superstition. Breaking free from the things that vary across cultures will mean subjecting the varying moral values to the rigors of science and reason. It is a proposal for overcoming the things that divide us in our world, uniting us to what Harris believes we all share regardless of culture: reason itself.

Harris crudely lumps a lot under the label "relativism," but he is right that there is a popular version of it that claims that if ethical behavior can be understood in terms of a culture or belief system (such as religion), it is beyond critique. This is a liberal, multicultural vision. But Žižek argues that this vision is especially problematic because when it acts as a principle for organizing a society, or when working across different societies, it falls into contradiction. "[I]t cannot stand on its own, it is parasitic upon some preceding form of what is usually referred to as 'socialization,' which it simultaneously undermines, thereby cutting off the branch on which it is sitting."[36] The liberal perspective that counsels respect for differing moral viewpoints is itself a moral viewpoint. The problem is that the liberal perspective cannot really admit this without losing the argument. It busily postpones an engagement with its own project *as itself a moral position*. The threat of cutting off the branch that supports liberalism keeps it from this engagement.

Admittedly, this is not quite the way that Harris argues against moral relativism. But it is crucial to see that he is not alone among contemporary thinkers. Even more crucial, though, is Harris's failure to abide himself by the same critiques that apply to his liberal opponents. In short, if relativists are vulnerable to criticism for holding an unacknowledged moral position of their own, thereby deluding themselves that their respect for socialized positions is not itself socialized, then those who make these critiques are *also* vulnerable to them. Everyone, it seems, wants to say that the particularities of history, culture, and language apply to others but not to themselves. For some, the way to transcend such variables is through liberal doctrine. For Harris, it is through science and reason.

The point I am making is that Harris only adopts skepticism when it suits him. He will consign his opponents' beliefs to culture and history, but not his own. In truth, he is wedded to a version of placing hope in reason that had its heyday several hundred years ago in the Age of Enlightenment (mid-seventeenth to late eighteenth century), when Western thought most credulously sought a universal morality through reason alone, when religion was thought to impede progress, and when science was thought to transcend culture. His ideas about reason and science are just as much the product of a particular, culture-bound style of thinking as are all ideas and all people. On its own, this does not invalidate his ideas any more than it invalidates any others'. But the fact that Sam Harris avoids this reality is telling. When it is pointed out, science and reason are brought back down to earth. Sorry, Sam, but that's where they have always been.

Belief and faith

Harris's own research in neuroscience involves what he calls the science of belief. In brain scans, the same regions of our brains are shown to be involved in believing matters of fact (the earth goes around the sun) and matters of value (it is wrong to torture the innocent). On this basis, Harris concludes that the brain does not distinguish between facts and values, meaning that neither should philosophy. And since we have a science of facts—physics, chemistry, and so on—we can likewise have a science of morality that will lead us to genuinely right answers to moral questions. I will have more to say in the next chapter about philosophy's long history of preserving the fact–value distinction that Harris wants to overcome. But when it comes to this point about how the brain works, he ought to be more modest about what this actually proves.

In his review of *The Moral Landscape* published in the *New York Review of Books*, biologist H. Allen Orr points out that these observations about the brain no more make facts and values identical than a brain scan that lights up in the same way when doing addition and multiplication would call into question the addition–multiplication distinction.[37] Likewise, it would be nonsense to suggest that scans showing that the brain behaves similarly when someone believes something true as when they believe something false somehow proves that there is no difference between truth and falsehood. It would merely show that when we believe something to be true—whether facts or values—our commitment to its truth is similar enough to involve the same part of the brain. Left out would be analysis of the beliefs themselves. Are they true or false? What makes them so? These more fundamental questions are not ones that neuroscience seems able to answer, even in principle.

More importantly, Harris doesn't acknowledge that we actually believe things for all kinds of reasons and that there are many different kinds of belief. Instead, readers are quickly shown options that are starkly black and white. "Either a person has good reasons for what he believes, or he does not." Christian beliefs are especially subjected to this clumsy, binary logic.

- "The Bible is either the word of God, or it isn't. Either Jesus offers humanity the one, true path to salvation (John 14.6), or he does not."

- "Either the Bible is just an ordinary book, written by mortals, or it isn't."
- "The choice before us is simple: we can either have a twenty-first century conversation about morality and human well-being [. . .] or we can confine ourselves to a first-century conversation as it is preserved in the Bible."

It goes without saying that this starkness is often artificial. When he says "Either Christ was divine, or he was not," Harris shows that he has neither the knowledge nor patience to discuss what Christianity has actually taught about the person of Christ for nearly two millennia.[38]

Setting aside specifically religious beliefs, consider the many things that we believe but are not able to prove. Consider history. Do I believe for good reasons or bad ones that Plato lived in Athens? I happen to trust the sources that say he did live there. Is my belief that the CIA was behind the 1961 assassination of the Congolese Prime Minster Patrice Lumumba justified or unjustified? Historians debate this; the evidence is impressive but not decisive.[39] Do the origins of capitalism reside in the ethic of Calvinism, as Max Weber famously argued? Scholars have tangled with this thesis for over a century.[40] Was the Great Library of Alexandria destroyed by Christians or is this accusation part of a much later myth? The facts appear to be less conclusive than what many critics of Christianity believe.[41] Was Neville Chamberlain merely weak in appeasing Hitler, as Winston Churchill claimed? Or, seeing that a war with Germany was inevitable, was he cleverly buying Britain time to build up its forces? Historians debate this too.[42] As it happens, nearly everything in history is up for debate.

It is simply not the case that, as Harris says, "Everyone recognizes that to rely upon 'faith' to decide specific questions of historical fact is ridiculous."[43] A lot of things have happened in the history of life on earth and I have been an eyewitness to only a very small fraction of them. If I believe that any of the rest of it happened, it is because I rely on what other people have said about it. Hopefully I can consult an eyewitness report. If there are conflicting reports, I will need to decide which ones are more reliable and trustworthy. If I read a history book, I may need to have a certain amount of trust in the scholar who wrote it; otherwise I should do the work myself. And why should I trust one scholar's work over another? And on and on.

Where in this process do we pass from justified belief to unjustified, blind faith? Probably somewhere. But very seldom can we have the clarity of Harris's sharp either–or. We believe things for all kinds of reasons. If I believe that my wife loves me, I can marshal what I consider some pretty good evidence for it. But it won't be incontrovertible—love calls for love in response. If there were proof, it wouldn't be love nor would love be a proper answer to it. While we trust some people for what we think are good reasons, others may not trust them for what they also consider good reasons. Differences like this are very hard to resolve even after all the evidence is in. There are some as yet undiscovered facts out there that no one believes (such as the existence of unobserved microorganisms). There are also some facts that are difficult to believe because they are too bizarre or unlikely (such as that the sun's mass bends space-time).

When we are asked to justify anything we believe, it would be comforting to be able simply to point to facts that speak for themselves. But this is not the way most things work. Instead, we can only point to the sources we trust. In this sense, *all belief rests on a kind of faith.* (Science is no exception to this, as I will discuss in the next chapter.)

Double standards and unanswered questions

Even though it grieves Harris that millions of people believe things on faith understood as insufficient evidence, his main worry is that this kind of belief is dangerous. He describes the bizarre story of Ria Ramkissoon, who starved her eighteen-month-old child for failing to say "Amen" after meals.

Ramkissoon negotiated a plea agreement that charges would be dropped in the event that the child is resurrected. This is a truly disturbing story about a young mother who was taken in by a religious cult. She is not insane, Harris says, but suffers from religion.[44]

To Harris, when people of faith do bad things, they discredit their faith. It is curious that Harris sets up Ramkissoon to represent all religious people; why not simply discredit Ramkissoon's One Mind Ministries? At any rate, I only want to show how quick he is to blame "religion" by citing her sanity. Harris applies a double standard to the moral accomplishments and failures of religious people compared with those of atheists.

When it comes to whole cultures, Harris would rather discuss Sweden and Denmark than avowedly atheist regimes such as China and the Soviet Union. He consistently points out that these Scandinavian societies outrank much more religious nations on matters like healthcare, economic equality, crime, and literacy. Is there a real correlation here? Among the many neglected factors, these are countries with a history of Christianity. What role does that history continue to play? Scholars show that, despite declines in church attendance, many social and political values are holdovers from Christianity. One scholar asks, "What is the source of the tolerance that characterizes modern Sweden, if not its cultural value core of which religion was the primary bearer?"[45] (Nietzsche's great concern was that people tend to cling to their moral convictions even when they stop going to church.)

These Scandinavian nations are also historically mono-racial and, thanks to an established church and even compulsory church attendance in some cases, have not faced conditions where one cultural religion has needed to define itself against another in order to establish or maintain identity (as has been in the case in, say, Northern Ireland and Poland[46]). It is doubtful that Harris would say that racial purity, much less religious uniformity, are key ingredients to social well-being.

What about when atheist dictators like Hitler and Stalin enact oppressive regimes? Harris considers them irrational or delusional.[47] In this, he relies on the classic "No True Scotsman" fallacy in which a counter-example is excluded rather than refuted. The term for this comes from the philosopher Antony Flew (1923–2010), who imagined a Scotsman's disbelief upon reading about a violent crime committed by another Scotsman. Because he can't very well claim "No Scotsman would do such a thing!" he revises his claim to be "No *true* Scotsman would do such a thing!"[48] In Harris's case, confronted with examples like Hitler and Stalin, he excludes them rather than refutes the argument, crying, "No *true* atheist would act so irrationally!"

James Wood, a sympathetic critic of Harris, explains why this argument fails to work. "This may be a little self-serving, in that 'reasonable' is here being defined by what it excludes: it cannot be reasonable to be a Nazi, and therefore Nazism is by definition unreasonable."[49] Many people avoid the case of Hitler by insisting that he must have been insane even though recent scholarship argues otherwise.[50] Harris's own solution is actually to blame religion for Hitler and other atheist tyrants. He says that theirs is not true atheism, but *dogmatic atheism*: "The problem with religion—as with Nazism, Stalinism, or any other totalitarian mythology—is the problem of dogma itself."[51]

Because Harris views *all* religious belief as dogmatic, there is little use in joining with religious people in opposing the dangers of "dogmatism." And the evil atheists? Because they are dogmatic in their atheism, they function as though they were religious! No one should accept this phony argument. (By the way, Harris works hard to show that when religious people show compassion their faith has nothing to do with it.[52])

When it comes to science itself, doesn't Harris owe readers an explanation of abuses done by and in the name of science? After all, it won't work simply to dismiss them with a "No true scientist!" argument. The world science has created has never been one of straightforward moral progress. In addition to antibiotics and air conditioning, science has also given us nuclear weapons, forced sterilizations, and eugenics. Clearly *some* scientists will conduct their craft according to the goal of seeking the well-being of others. But some won't. And if science doesn't provide the principle of seeking well-being (as Harris admits), where are the controlling moral principles to be found?

Furthermore, is science able to save itself from its own excesses? Who corrects science? Why isn't it self-correcting? What else is corrupting it? What else does it need? Must scientists be moral or is it enough that they simply be good scientists?[53]

If science is being promoted as the key to human happiness, we also deserve some accounting of the genuine disasters science has produced even with the best of intentions. Consider technologies that were once thought successful but were later declared disasters. For example, the drug Thalidomide, prescribed to treat morning sickness in pregnant women in the late 1950s, was stopped after it was linked to thousands of severe birth defects.

Paul Virilio, a French social theorist, writes that along with every invention comes the invention of an *accident* related to it. The invention of the locomotive is also the invention of the derailment; the invention of the stock market is also the invention of the stock market crash; the ship, the shipwreck; the nuclear reactor, nuclear waste.[54] We can even become blinded to some problems by the solutions we invented in solving other ones.

There are also *moral* accidents. Which moral problems and unanswered moral questions have been created by science as it sought to create a better world? What does an irresponsible pharmaceutical company owe to Thalidomide's victims? How can we as a species learn to live in a world where so much suffering is our own invention? How can the scientific community continue to go on in the face of failure? I will not pretend that these questions have easy answers. But it is remarkable that they have no place on Harris's moral landscape.

*

We've looked in this chapter at the shape of Harris's program for morality and have briefly considered how it is connected with his critiques of religion and faith. It is appropriate to have concluded the chapter with some of the kinds of questions that science and reason seem ill-equipped to answer. I have begun to gesture toward what I consider to be a richer set of moral considerations. These will be developed more in later chapters as we take up more and more explicitly theological themes. But if science and reason aren't all that some people take them to be—objective, universal, and purely evidence-based—then it is advisable to learn to spot their distinctive style of hubris.

2

The arrogance of reason

In my experience, arrogance is about as common at a scientific conference as nudity.

Sam Harris, *The Moral Landscape*[1]

[T]here have been some extraordinarily arrogant scientists.

Sam Harris, *Letter to a Christian Nation*[2]

Traditionally, when a deformed child was born among the Nuer tribe in South Sudan, it would be taken away from the village and set in a river where it would die. They believed that such a child was not a Nuer. It was really a hippopotamus and ought to go live with its own kind. The Nuer were not faced with any difficult moral questions. They did not puzzle about the ethics of infanticide. The only real dilemma would arise if a mother decided she wanted to keep her newborn hippopotamus.[3]

Clearly not everyone seeks the well-being of conscious creatures. Even when they do, they don't always seek it in the same ways. They may even disagree on what a human creature is. Harris strongly opposes the kind of relativistic viewpoint that concludes that the Nuer are not morally to blame for the deaths of these children because they are only being true to their understanding of the world. Since science can tell us that an infant, however deformed, is a human rather than a hippo, the Nuer are working with deluded beliefs—rather than genuine facts—about the world. This seems to be a case where science presents us with findings about the way the world *is* (deformed babies are still human) and there are ways of acting that *ought* to follow from this information.

Notice how "is" and "ought" function in the previous sentence. It is the difference between what *is* the case and what *should be* the case. There appears to be a natural movement from is to ought, from facts about the world to normative moral values and behavior. Harris believes science and morality to be related in just this way. This is why he speaks about a science of morality.

In technical terms, Harris defends a viewpoint called *moral realism*: just as there are facts about other things, there are also moral facts, some of which are true. If we can test questions we have about nutrition, we can also test questions we have about right and wrong. On Harris's account, true moral claims have their source in facts about our world. And our knowledge of these facts is provided by empirical science. We can ask whether acting one way rather than another increases human happiness and well-being, or whether it causes human suffering. When we do this, Harris notes that we are asking about matters that are both empirical and moral.

The implication is that if the Nuer got their facts about humans and hippos straight, they would be prepared to make better ethical choices concerning newborns. In the meantime, those who have the facts that the Nuer don't have are justified when they condemn this practice of abandoning infants. As Harris says,

> It seems to me patently obvious that we can no more respect and tolerate vast differences in notions of human well-being than we can respect or tolerate vast differences in the notions about how disease spreads, or in the safety standards of buildings and airplanes.[4]

All such things are envisioned to be factual in the same way.

The *is* and *ought* of well-being

Is it possible to move from facts to values in quite this way? For centuries, moral philosophers have doubted it. Even New Atheist celebrity Richard Dawkins admits that while it can clarify important ethical questions, "science has no methods for deciding what is ethical."[5] Yet in recent decades, others have followed the lead of famed biologist E. O. Wilson, whose book *Sociobiology: The New Synthesis* (1975) sought biological explanations for questions long thought to belong to other disciplines. As Wilson puts it, "Ought is the product of a material process." Any statement of value is "just shorthand for one kind of factual statement."[6] Harris's project follows Wilson in his determination to overcome the is–ought distinction. But it is questionable whether it is possible to overcome this distinction.

Before going further, I should admit that in arguing against Harris on this point, I have no particular stake in upholding this distinction. If David Hume, the eighteenth-century Scottish philosopher most associated with it, should turn out to be mistaken, so be it. After all, many statements of fact such as "Your car is being towed" strongly suggest some action that ought to be taken.

Even so, when it comes to weightier matters, there will always be better and worse descriptions of the way things are. Have we truly accounted for everything relevant to *is* when we then attempt to move on to *ought*? If the world belongs to God, then however we describe other facts about the world should be bound up with this claim. Philosophers and theologians have often debated whether one can logically move from "God exists" to "God ought to be obeyed." It is a worthy question but there is a prior one. After all, neither Harris nor Hume believes that God exists or that the world belongs to God, so we already disagree about what *is*. (Ethicist Jeffrey Stout suggests a thought experiment: imagine two possible worlds but God only exists in one of them. Stout argues that the same acts will be considered good in both worlds.[7] I think Stout has got it wrong. A lot depends on what we mean by "God.") As I will go on to argue below, how we describe what *is* is already shaped by our values. But that argument will have to wait.

The well-being (often *global* well-being) of conscious creatures is Harris's guiding moral principle. It is a different principle from Wilson's, though. Wilson taught that biology helps us understand human action as based in the attempt to pass on our DNA in the world—this is meant to explain procreation and aggression in self-defense; it also explains self-sacrifice aimed at the survival of one's offspring. In looking to enrich the well-being of all, Harris isn't looking for these kinds of more direct clues from biology. Still, if he is to succeed in overcoming the is–ought distinction, well-being will have to pass the same test that Wilson believed he himself had passed; it will have to be both *is* and *ought*. More specifically, well-being will have to be an *is* before it is an *ought*. He will have to show that moral values framed in terms of well-being follow from observable facts about the world.

Is it enough to agree that well-being is better than its opposite? Of course people in most circumstances will seek to promote their own well-being. But what says that they *ought to* seek the well-being of others, especially strangers across the globe? Might they instead focus on the well-being of those closest to themselves—their friends and family? It turns out that Harris never says why people ought to seek the well-being of others. Missing is any scientific finding whatsoever that would lead to his conclusion. It is not a promising place to begin.

In a review of *The Moral Landscape*, Russell Blackford identifies this problem in Harris's account of global well-being. Blackford, who is editor-in-chief of the *Journal of Evolution and Technology*, argues that the single principle that Harris depends on so heavily—the principle of global well-being—is a value we are told we *ought* to have even while it is something for which Harris provides no evidence. "If we presuppose the well-being of conscious creatures as a fundamental value, much else may fall into place, but that initial presupposition does not come from science. It is not an empirical finding."[8] Likewise, Peter Singer, possibly the most influential living ethicist, thinks this is the biggest problem with Harris's project. While science can help us decide what to do—how best to act on moral principles—it cannot *provide* us with those principles.[9]

Anticipating this critique, Harris simply dismisses it. He claims that if someone doesn't already see why well-being is to be valued, there is no point arguing it. According to Blackford, this illustrates that Harris is actually relying on a value (an *ought*) rather than a fact about the world (an *is*) at the precise point where his theory most needs to avoid this. Consider how it would work in practice.

Imagine you are trying to convince your neighbor to recycle her empty bottles. Perhaps you know the facts better than your neighbor does when it comes to the harm that not doing so has on the environment. Along with these facts, you appeal to the global well-being of conscious creatures and the planet they share that is so necessary for their well-being. But your neighbor knows the landfill is far away and prefers the convenience of tossing bottles into the trash along with everything else. In the end, she is unmoved by your exhortation about global well-being.

What shall we make of this example? Is your neighbor being less than consummately moral? Almost certainly. Is she mistaken about the world in some way? No. Her "What's it to me?" attitude, as Blackford characterizes it, will provoke disapproval in some. But the reason for this disapproval will have nothing to do with claims about her irrationality or ignorance of scientific data. It will be that she doesn't value the global well-being of conscious creatures as she ought. And why ought she to value this? Harris is no help here. Blackford is right: Harris succeeds no better than anyone else has in getting *ought* from *is*.[10]

If it were possible in every instance, we would find it much easier to point to scientific facts about the world when we wanted to settle disagreements on moral matters. This is Harris's goal, so much so that he describes his concept of well-being as "the only thing we can reasonably value."[11] Valuing anything else is irrational. But it should be obvious that people may still disagree about values even when all the facts are in. When this happens, we will need more than science alone to arbitrate the disagreement. Short of resolving things, we will make arguments as best we can and attempt to persuade those with whom we differ.

Harris concedes that his idea of well-being is difficult to define. It's fuzzy around the edges, much like the word "health." Yet he insists that, like health, just because it is hard to define doesn't make it useless. We still find it useful to recommend exercise and proper nutrition because they are good for our bodies even though a rigorous and comprehensive description of health eludes us. In defending this analogy to critics, though, he reintroduces the very distinction he intends to overcome—that between *is* and *ought*. "There is still an objective reality to which our beliefs about human health can correspond. Questions of 'should' are not the right lens through which to see this."[12] In having to admit to using what we *should* do as a premise rather than a conclusion, but being unable to demonstrate that that premise arises from objective reality, he now seems forced to back away from it.

Specifically responding to Blackford on this point, Harris concedes that science cannot establish his premise about seeking well-being. Curiously, he continues to argue that it doesn't matter:

Again, the same can be said about medicine, or science as a whole. As I point out in my book, science is based on values that must be presupposed—like the desire to understand the universe, a respect for evidence and logical coherence, etc. One who doesn't share these values cannot do science. But nor can he attack the presuppositions of science in a way that anyone should find compelling. Scientists need not apologize for presupposing the value of evidence, nor does this presupposition render science unscientific.[13]

There is something religious—at least as far as Harris conceives of religion—in this appeal to core beliefs that science cannot demonstrate. But it also sounds like the confession of a guilty secret. In searching his writings, I have found that Harris is almost never this forthcoming about science's lack of indubitable foundations. When he describes religion in these terms, for example, it is a scandal. A great deal of philosophy, including philosophy of science, has reflected on the fact that we always seem to begin unfounded and in the middle. This line of thinking has sometimes made science honest about its own limits and realistic about its promises and aims. Harris appears to conclude the opposite: because his science of morality is just as unfounded as all science, it is permitted to strike out on a world-saving mission with arrant boldness.

Good life / bad life

Supposing people in the West were to take stock of the *benefits* of science, there are too many to name. When it comes to technology, consider that an estimated 30 million mobile phone users make 132 million calls in the United Kingdom every day. In the United States, around 2.4 billion calls are made on 300 million mobile phones. Why mention mobile phones? Strangely enough, they are a key to uncovering some serious flaws in Harris's account.

To make a convincing case that science can address the topic of morality, Harris paints two strongly contrasting pictures—what he calls the Good Life and the Bad Life. He need only persuade readers that anyone would judge the one better than the other and that the most pressing questions involve how to move oneself or others from the Bad Life to the Good Life. Harris does not mean for them to be models or patterns, but as extreme poles at either end of a continuum, ones that any reasonable person would accept without dispute as manifestly good and bad. But probably unwittingly, Harris ends up revealing much more than this.

Let's first look at how he paints the Good Life. It is a happily married couple who enjoy a dual income, apparently no children, and are the successful recipients of a billion-dollar grant to fund their charity. This life, especially owing to "wealth and social connections," provides the couple unmitigated enjoyment of leisure and meaningful work.[14] But in a shockingly revealing omission, Harris neglects to say that in the real world, no one can live this Good Life if there do not also exist millions who live the Bad Life. As I will go on to argue further, I do not simply mean this in the sense that the "less fortunate" provide ample opportunity for this couple to experience happiness through helping them. For the moment, though, there is also the Bad Life to consider.

The Bad Life is clearly one that no one would choose. In a war-torn nation, a young widow flees from her pursuers. The child soldiers wield machetes, rape, terrify, and murder the inhabitants of the village. It is such an overwhelming combination of unlivable factors that calling it the Bad Life scarcely covers it.

Guided by the task of improving the widow's life—of moving the Bad Life closer to the Good Life in any respect whatsoever—Harris wants to argue that any person has what they need to begin thinking morally about it. His point is not that science and reason will tell us specifically how to do it. It is that there is something indisputable about calling one "good" and other one "bad." We don't need to slip into fuzzy language that takes us away from things as they are in the real world. For Harris, there are objective differences that uncontroversially involve facts about the way things are. The difference in well-being that these two images present is, Harris contends, entirely objective. Yet if we press these images a bit and make them more concrete than Harris intends, it is easy to notice some assumptions he makes that, in the end, are severely damaging to his project as a whole.

For one thing, even though Harris does not say it, we know that horrific things like these have been going on for the past decade in the Democratic Republic of the Congo, especially in the eastern regions near the border with Rwanda. I find that many of my students have never heard about the war, which was at its height between 1998 and 2004. Yet even though many people in the West do not hear about the war in the Congo and its related causalities often enough to remind them about it, it is the deadliest conflict since the Second World War.

Can we conclude anything from the fact that the war in the Congo generally elicits very little objective response from much of the world's population even when they do know about it? This question is at the heart of an extraordinary video documentary by Eric Metzgar called *The Reporter*. In it, Metzgar accompanies *New York Times* columnist Nicholas Kristof to remote regions of the Congo, into the heart of the ongoing war. In the course of their travels, Kristof's reporting technique begins to unnerve Metzgar. The reporter consistently and relentlessly seeks out the most extreme and heart-wrenching stories of human suffering. He knows that his Western readers are well-practiced at protecting their consciences. It is very difficult to move them emotionally. But by sharing the most grisly rape story he can find, Kristof reasons that he might be able to break through to a desensitized audience.

I believe Kristof is bumping up against a serious flaw in Harris's argument. The war in the Congo is real and continues to cause great human suffering, claiming more lives than the Holocaust. Harris is quite right that such conflicts bring about the exact opposite of human well-being; they bring about the

Bad Life. Yet the misery continues. Why? We do not suffer from religious delusions clouding our moral responsibilities (religion is Harris's first target). Nor is there any lack of clarity about the fact that the millions forced to endure the war's ravages are living the Bad Life, to say the least (moral relativism and liberalism are Harris's second targets). It is a triumph of science and reason to declare that seeking human well-being in the Congo is a moral response to that tragedy—a *meager* response, we might say. But it is not enough. As humans, our problems are much deeper. How so?

Both Harris and Metzgar discuss the phenomenon of "psychic numbing." Drawing on the research of psychologist Paul Slovic, they explain what happens when test subjects are confronted with varying numbers of human lives that are being threatened. Faced with a single human being, subjects exhibit the greatest concern; however, their concern drastically diminishes as the numbers rise. When presented with an entire civilization under grave threat, people exhibit what Slovic calls "genocide neglect"—we shut down emotionally and practically. Harris says this is a moral failing of people and a "startling limitation on our capacity for moral reasoning."[15] I agree. But it is not at all clear that this is an insight that science and reason alone provide us.

Why not rather conclude that the human phenomenon of genocide neglect is a genuine finding of science that ought to round out our moral knowledge of the way things are? After all, one might be thought completely *rational* to be overwhelmed by vast suffering, wondering "What good can I do?" and lamenting "I am just one person." Harris does not even entertain the possibility. It is, instead, an *irrational* human response and therefore "an obvious violation of moral norms."[16] If we at first fail to respond emotionally and practically, Harris has astounding confidence that human reason will see to it that we come around to "our better selves." I believe history shows this is not very likely.

A world without mobile phones?

I will raise three major objections. First, Harris's image of the Good Life depends on some—millions, in fact—living the Bad Life. The leisure lifestyle of the affluent, suburban couple with "good genes and optimal circumstances" has an underside, as a moment's reflection reveals. To maintain it, they depend on others doing such disagreeable work as driving the truck containing their household's garbage to a landfill and mining the minerals that go into their computers and phones. At the least, it's a lifestyle that we would need to demote on the Good–Bad scale if the couple were to take upon themselves some of these duties. And wouldn't the Good Life need to be demoted in just this way for *anyone* nearer the other end to slide closer and closer to Good?[17]

So it is not the case that, as Harris imagines, he has painted a picture of the Good Life that would simply need to be dangled before any reasonable person's eyes in order to get them to tap into their moral selves as they yearn after greater well-being. Far from it. In fact, we have a *symptom* of a world that injustice has created—where some are rich because others are poor. Worse still, Harris is asking readers to accept that "nothing [is] more important, at least for ourselves and for those closest to us, than the difference between the Bad Life and the Good Life."[18] Yet this difference always comes at a cost.

To make things even more concrete: it is one thing to say you can imagine a world without suffering and misery; but can you imagine a world devoid of mobile phones? Many consumer electronic products, including mobile phones, use the mineral coltan in their circuitry. The Congo holds an estimated 80 percent of this highly sought after mineral that links the Good Life and the Bad Life. A 2003 United Nations investigation revealed seventy global companies trading in minerals sourced in the Congo. The war there was shown to be connected to the world economy through trade lines and practices of numerous European, American, and Asian businesses.[19] In the Congo, the UN team followed up on rumors of planeloads of coltan being smuggled into neighboring Rwanda. They found extensive looting, sourcing, and transporting by both local defense and rebel groups. The coltan trade was especially a boon for the Rwanda-backed rebel group RCD (Rassemblement Congolais pour la Démocratie) operating in the Congo. In 2000, the RCD was able to become self-sustaining in its military operations as a result, turning an estimated profit of $30 million from exploited mineral trading in that year.[20] The consumer demand for coltan has been directly tied to exploitation of natural resources and ravages of human populations in eastern Congo. It is therefore tied to the Bad Life.

My point is not that a world without mobile phones will automatically be a more peaceful world. It is that advancing people from the Bad Life closer to the Good Life will require sacrifices from affluent people and nations. The question is therefore simple: can science alone move anyone to make such sacrifices? (Recall the Good-Life couple who administer charities with billion-dollar grants. It is other people's money; their charity costs them nothing.)

My second point has to do with "psychic numbing"—the increasing human insensitivity as far-off atrocities grow in scale. To overcome this, Harris commends working *against* something to which it seems we are naturally inclined. Why can doing so seem perfectly moral? The reason is one that Harris does not notice: only those powerful and influential enough to do some practical and measurable good in the face of vast suffering are in the position to act "rationally" to overcome psychic numbing. At a deeper level, this reveals the way that Harris is actually encoding the cultural supremacy of the West in what he labels "rational" and therefore "moral."

It is important not to miss the imperialist assumption that the Congo example reveals. It is, I believe, a perspective that Harris holds without even being aware of it: that moral questions are faced only by power-holders and decision-makers.

This "morality from above" hardly notices who is left out of the discussion, in this case the Congolese woman herself. What are *her* moral questions and how ought she answer them? How should she employ science and reason? The reason Harris doesn't say is that she is entirely left out of his thesis and his book, except as the recipient of aid from people with power and means. Harris assumes that the moral landscape that science informs, and on occasion yields, is serviceable only to people who are in positions to improve the well-being of others.

In looking at actual history, we would see precisely what this has meant. Wealthy people—and especially wealthy nations—have assumed the responsibility to provide the rest of the world with the moral norms. As I will go on to argue later in this chapter, this paternalistic perspective is nothing new. Nor is it (as Harris mistakenly takes for granted) what one is automatically left holding on to once one dismisses moral relativism.

My third point is a theological one: as Christian thought has nearly always insisted, the human problem is much more profound and troublesome than ignorance or irrationality. Our problem is a corrupted will. We want the wrong things. If the doctor scolds you for not exercising or the dentist reprimands you for not flossing your teeth, it's not because you don't know how to do it or haven't already been told thousands of times that you should. Knowing more only takes us so far—it won't save your pearly whites or your waistline. Will knowing the right thing spur us on to make changes in how we live? Will it help us surrender our own well-being for the sake of others? In short, can knowing the right thing provide us with the moral courage to follow through on it?

Here is what I mean: most Christian thinking has followed Augustine, the fifth-century theologian, who taught that sin is much more like addiction than poor choices. When Christians speak about the human condition being marred by sin, they have in mind a much more serious reality than the mere fact that we are prone to make bad choices based on poor information. Harris discusses a friend's young daughter who, through conversation with her father, begins to question the connection between the well-being of the lamb she is eating and her own lamb-eating enjoyment. Her conclusion is eminently human: the situation is far from good, but she can't stop eating lambs if people keep killing them for people like her.[21] Harris comments that "it can be difficult to do what one believes to be right on one's own." Revealingly, he goes on to admit that this may even be impossible and that science may not help us practically; he only wants to defend this part of his thesis in theory.

Yet it is a thoroughly Augustinian point that Paul also wrestles with in his New Testament Letter to the Romans. You can sense his own confusion when he writes, "I can will what is right, but I cannot do it. For I do not do the good I want, but the evil I do not want is what I do" (Romans 7.18–19). Immorality runs much deeper than our ignorance; it affects our will. So then we are not simply poor and ignorant decision-makers, we are *addicts* no different from the little girl who cannot stop eating lamb, even with her new information. Therefore, it seems that Harris has said far too little. Reason alone will surely do *some* of what Harris says. It may provide us with the bland conclusion that not-suffering is better than suffering. When faced with an example of a suffering person living the Bad Life, we can all agree that we would much prefer something better—not only for ourselves but also for her. But can science and reason take us any further?

After all, it is one thing to want to ease the suffering of the Congolese woman. It is quite another thing to curb the consumer habits of affluent societies whose ways of living have come to depend so crucially on minerals from the Congo. Explaining the rationality of doing so is likely to produce little effect. Why is this? If we can't rely on reason alone to do this, what is missing? Can science bend our wills? Can it heal the wounds of perversity and depravity that mark humanity?

Augustine had a far more realistic grasp of the human potential and tendency for evil than does Harris. Augustine diagnosed the human problem as being located in our deformed wills. What if I am unwilling to change my life in any serious ways to improve the well-being of others across the globe? I may even have learned a great deal about their suffering, yet I remain stuck in my lifestyle addicted to consumer electronics. Can science make me moral? I do not suffer from lack of knowledge, but lack of will.[22]

Shutting down debate

Much more could be said about well-being and the good life. But I trust I have said enough to show that, while Harris makes it sound as though he is locating morality in science (this is the central thesis of *The Moral Landscape*), in fact he is doing nothing of the sort. What is he doing instead? The answer, as it happens, is much more conventional and a lot less interesting than what he claims:

1   Harris takes for granted, rather than shows, that "the well-being of conscious creatures" ought to be the governing, universal ethic that every person should adopt.
2   Then he shows how science can help to bring about well-being.

Notice what is happening here. This way of arguing skips over the moral questions entirely, thereby avoiding the heart of the matter. This leads him to do a mild reversal after 1 and 2. He insists that whatever we thought we meant by words like "morality" ought to be exclusively described using the findings of science. Morality now simply *means* whatever contributes to global well-being. Well-being, in turn, simply *means* the kinds of states that science can say something about.

This last move is especially important. On Harris's account, religious morality is discounted because its concern for well-being is supernatural and otherworldly. Religious "precepts often have nothing to do with maximizing well-being in *this* world."[23] They can therefore support actions that actually bring about greater human misery, postponing the alleviation of suffering beyond this life. Sadly, much of this is true of how religious morality has actually functioned. Yet notice that Harris's account of morality does not merely point to empirical failures of religions throughout the ages. It actually depends on religious claims not being true. If, for example, the care of eternal souls should not be a moral factor, it is not because such care has nothing to do with human well-being. It is just that the idea of eternal souls is *false*—a religious fantasy and delusion.

Harris can then propound his circular maxim: well-being is what morality is all about, and since everything about well-being falls within the domain of science and not religion, science alone determines morality. It is a clever trick, perhaps, but it is only a trick. It is sleight of hand. But it is only a particularly brazen example of a more general overreach strategy that silences and ignores opposing viewpoints without engagement.

Consider the concrete example of embryonic stem-cell research that Harris discusses. Research of this kind potentially holds enormous promise for treating many debilitating diseases such as Parkinson's. However, opponents of using human embryonic stem-cells in scientific research object to the fact that it involves the destruction of human embryos. Focusing exclusively on the potential increase in the well-being of stem-cell therapy patients, Harris thinks that showing concern about human embryos is "one of the many delusional products of religion that has led to an ethical blind alley, and to terrible failures of compassion."[24] The Catholic Church, and those who agree with it, is accused of immorality.

Harris sees no reason to be concerned that embryos are human beings at a very early stage and ought to be protected. The reason? "Because almost every cell in your body is a potential human being, given our recent advances in genetic engineering."[25] This argument has the form: since science can now do X (which may or may not be moral), then there is no moral reason to keep from doing Y. Science doesn't settle the moral question—it creates it! Mocking the language of "souls," Harris makes the mistake of thinking that Christians and others who use the term are stepping on science's toes. It is as if, because a soul is not an organ, there is no sense in talking about it. Never mind the ancient Greek idea that the soul is the form of the body (rather than an object within it, which probably no one believes). It is possible to argue, using this understanding of souls, that a blastocyst is unformed and therefore not yet "souled." But the alternative to dispensing with the "naive idea of souls in a Petri dish" appears to be a perfect disregard of questions about the moral status of early human life as well as ridicule for anyone who thinks they are worth asking.[26] As far as Harris is concerned, there is no ethical debate to be had. Religious worries needlessly complicate a matter that is "utterly straightforward."[27]

It seems to me that this is a debate that is at least worth having and we should all be skeptical of those who simply want to shut it down. Recall the Nuer tribe who think that deformed babies are hippos. Remember that there is no ethical debate for them when it comes to the fate of these newborns. For them, the situation is "utterly straightforward." It is not likely that Harris would argue that showing concern for them is delusional. But why not? Science tells us that human embryos are human just as much as it can show that baby Nuer are human. Does science go further to settle the moral question about what we *ought* to do with these facts? No it does not. Much of the debate over the use of human embryos in research turns on whether embryos have the same moral status as humans have at later stages of development. However, this is not a question that science can answer (although Harris tries to, comparing the moral status of a human embryo to that of a dead person![28]).

We can certainly point to the well-being of patients who would benefit from stem-cell therapy. But it is only by bracketing out other facts, such as the humanity of the embryos, that anyone can get away with thinking that the ethics of stem-cell research is "utterly straightforward."

Notice what Harris's approach is in this case. It is to shut down ethical debate by insisting that there is merely a single consideration, namely, the benefit to patients. But it is a debate that is worth having, if only because society is better served by having it than by avoiding it. Is it conceivable that we might, on occasion, be faced with moral choices that require us to stop going down one road, even when it leads to the well-being of some, because we have had to take into account other moral factors? An analogy can be seen in the ethics of war.

Centuries of Just War tradition condemn direct attacks on non-combatants even if a military objective can be reached sooner and with fewer total casualties. President Truman, for example, famously spurned Just War theory when he justified dropping atomic bombs on Japan in 1945. Bombing Japan might have increased total global well-being, not least because it ended the war. But most ethicists judge the bombing to be immoral, acknowledging that there are more factors to consider. For instance, how does intentionally targeting civilians corrupt the *perpetrators* and *their society*?

In the same way, a significant set of questions in the stem-cell debate has to do with what kind of society we want to be. If stem-cell research progresses as so many hope it will, there is no question that it will achieve enormous well-being for many. Yet will we become a culture that, in the process, ironically cheapens the value of nascent life? Who must a people become (or who are they already) who can so disregard the sacrifice of human embryos that doing so ceases even to register as a moral factor?

Harris elsewhere acknowledges this kind of consideration, although it plays no role in his discussion of human embryos. In discussing a well-known example by ethicist Peter Singer,

Harris agrees that we have a moral obligation to prevent something very bad from happening so long as we can do it without acting immorally. In Singer's example, if you see a child drowning in a shallow pond, you have a moral obligation to help. But Harris disagrees with Singer that this obligation is equivalent to responding to an appeal by a poverty-fighting charity organization.

> We all know that it would take a very different kind of person to walk past a child drowning in a shallow pond, out of concern for getting one's suit wet, than it takes to ignore an appeal from UNICEF. It says much more about you if you can walk past that pond. If we were all this sort of person, there would be terrible ramifications as far as the eye can see. It seems to me, therefore, that the challenge is to get clear about what the actual consequences of an action are, about what changes in human experience are possible, and about which changes matter.[29]

What "actual consequences" might Harris have in mind? Perhaps the hardness of heart a person must generate in order to sleep well at night, having left the child to drown. Becoming a morally insensitive person could take some time and effort. In addition to asking about the well-being of drowning and starving children, I think Harris is right to bring up this kind of real-world consideration of what it is like to be a person making a moral choice. Yet when it comes to the use of human embryos in scientific research, Harris curiously fixes on a single factor—the well-being of potential patients—while deriding as religious superstition concern over nascent human life on the grounds that such embryos are extremely small.

My point is not to try to settle the ethical controversy over stem-cell research. I only want to highlight Harris's dangerous tendency toward simplifying debates in order to taunt those who think the debates are actually more complex. This strategy seeks to win arguments without having to engage with them at all. It neither does justice to our rationality nor does it enhance a society's long-term well-being. So let us ask what has been left out.

Universal reason in crisis

Can science provide us with a universal morality that transcends the particularities of culture? It is more than carelessness that leads critics like Harris to focus on some things to the exclusion of others. It is not poor scholarship alone that results in a tendency to simplify complex questions of morality, reducing them until the answer appears obvious, with no argument necessary. The reduction of all religions to "religion," all religion to "faith," and all faith to unfounded certainty is not simply negligence.

As I will argue in this section, this phenomenon is what one should expect when values are thought to be objective moral facts, illuminated solely by the light of science and reason. Harris has things backward: rather than moral values being determined by facts about the world, what we call facts are actually deeply shaped by the things we already value.

One can easily see this in how science is actually conducted. Harris clings to a mythological account of science as objective and impartial, as transcending culture. Indeed, his readiness to criticize the irrationality and immorality of cultures other than his own depends on this mythology. In practice, science is rife with prior assumptions, preconceptions, ideological commitments, and articles of faith.

Science reflects the time and culture in which it is conducted. At a basic level, the methods, language, and units of measurement used in research partially set the terms for understanding and communicating the results. For example, research shows that the psychopathology of schizophrenia varies from culture to culture and may not be best explained by looking only at the brain. Because schizophrenia is almost completely unknown in primitive cultures, some are linking it to Western societies in which people must adapt artificially to widespread cultures of loneliness.[30] If scientists didn't think to look at cultural factors, but only looked at the brain, they would overlook this. Sometimes the cultural setting of the research itself sways research findings. For instance, between 1966 and 1995, all clinical trials conducted in three countries where acupuncture is common (China, Taiwan, Japan) showed that it is an effective treatment. But during the same period, only 56 percent of trials in the United States, Sweden, and the UK showed it to be effective.[31]

More generally, science is always motivated to ask some questions rather than others. Very often science will respond to what the wider society considers the hot-button issues of the day. The efforts of New Atheist scientists like Harris and Richard Dawkins openly reflect post-9/11 anxieties. The project of meeting these anxieties with an objectivity that supports the superiority of the West against the Muslim world flows from a specific interpretation of recent cultural and historical events. Its science is driven, at least in part, by fear of terrorism.

There are many more examples of culture determining scientific practice. Funding and government grants ensure that research will be conducted in some areas and not in others. In the United States, it is widely suspected that big business interests within the Department of Agriculture, rather than pure science, lie behind official policies and nutrition standards (ensuring the presence of the dairy industry in children's school lunches, for example). Since there is a lot more money in treating heart disease rather than preventing it, scientific resources are marshaled accordingly. Lung cancer kills many more Americans than breast cancer, yet it receives a fraction of the funding.[32] Breast cancer awareness groups do a better job than other groups; science commits itself accordingly.[33] As is the case everywhere, money talks.

In fact, money is essential to understanding how science works in our world. Some scientists have the personal means to promote their own work, while others don't (Harris personally helped to bankroll the $200,000 marketing budget for *Letter to a Christian Nation*[34]). Celebrity scientists play to their popular base and their fame owes as much to rhetorical skill, connections, hard cash, and knowing the concerns of their audience as it does to the truth of the science they promote. Desire for professional recognition and praise may also spur individual scientists along in their inquiries. Their findings are subject to the mediating culture of peer-review for permitting them to be considered, in Michel Foucault's phrase, "in the truth," even though the sheer number of scientific papers means that most findings go untested by others. There are also well-documented phenomena like publishing bias (in which scientific journals tend to prefer results that prove something positively rather than disprove negatively) and the selective reporting of results (in which scientists pick and choose some data over others for reporting based on what they are trying to show).[35] The ways that scientists perceive and investigate matters of truth and fact are closely tied to their culture. Only a mythic objectivity allows science to rise above it all. But it is just a self-serving myth.

The hope for a universal morality based on science simply cannot ignore these realities about how science is conducted. But Harris does ignore them. He barely contains his disdain for the entire science of anthropology for how irrational and immoral behaviors of cultures "have been rationalized, or even idealized, in the fire-lit scribblings of one or another dazzled ethnographer."[36] He blames anthropology for inventing and promoting cultural relativism rather than the fearless lack of respect that he thinks these degenerate cultural practices deserve. (It is worth noticing how selective Harris is about what he believes counts as true science.) So it is not surprising that his assembly of facts about our world quite simply exclude *all* observations about how science actually functions in the real world, from how big pharmaceutical companies work to how weapons research contracts are awarded. So much for the idea that science is strictly universal; what about morality?

If we had to pick one theme that has most occupied professional ethicists in the last three hundred years, we might choose the idea of a universal morality. If there was a single dream that the Enlightenment prized above all else, it was this one. Harris shares a centuries-old, albeit much discredited, philosophical ambition. Is there a single morality to which all thinking humans should ultimately subscribe? If so, what is its source? As we saw in the last chapter, the answer for Enlightenment philosophy was always *reason*.

Appealing to reason, the eighteenth-century philosopher Immanuel Kant (1724–1804) sought a universal moral code that everyone could (and should) subscribe to regardless of the particulars of their existence. Yet it is said that Kant never left his Prussian hometown of Königsberg and that he remained ignorant of what the new science of anthropology was beginning to say about other cultures. So he mistakenly thought of his own bourgeois morality as being universal. Jeremy Bentham (1748–1832), another Enlightenment philosopher, claimed that he could have run all of India from the comfort of his study, revealing how extraordinary his belief was that people are the same everywhere, that human reason and social harmony are universals.[37]

What is most striking about the Enlightenment project is its scorn for tradition. It scorned both particular traditions and the idea of tradition itself. Kant famously asked "What is Enlightenment?" and answered: "man's emergence from his self-incurred immaturity" and the courage "to use one's own understanding without the guidance of another."[38] *Sapere aude!* was a slogan—*Dare to be wise!* Many Enlightenment thinkers saw tradition as a threat to the universals they were discovering. Their confident dismissal placed unprecedented value on skepticism and novelty, producing sweeping claims about the capacities of reason and the achievement of distance from petty superstition.

The Enlightenment produced an enormous amount of philosophical, scientific, and literary sophistication. The problem is that it also produced incompatible universals. Kant and Bentham, for example, represent two very different ethical schools of thought (deontology and utilitarianism), both of which claim to be universal moralities. For contemporary philosophers like Alasdair MacIntyre, these so-called universals were bluffs waiting to be called. To call their bluff, all one needed to do was to point out the fact of competing universals. It's true that one might have been right and the other wrong. But several hundred years of philosophy has not confirmed the faith of those who thought that the steady march of progress would eventually show that one is more rational—and hence universal.

Especially in the last half-century, scholars have shown that in addition to the obvious variables between traditions, the "harder" sciences are likewise not the universals they purported to be. Mathematics, logic, and reason itself have all been shown to reflect the cultural contexts in which they arise. They vary across traditions.[39]

Harris's project should be understood within this context. He is keeping alive the Enlightenment dream and putting all of his stock into empirical science. This is not a new move by any means. The specifics of his project tend to side more with Bentham than with Kant, but he shares with both thinkers a hope for a universal morality.

It is important to recall the sense of urgency at work for those who dream this way. Rather than disagreeing interminably with each other, we might actually come to agreement. And where there is agreement, we are more likely to have concord and societal peace. Where moral disagreement has sometimes set people of different ethnic heritages and religious traditions at each other's throats, a universal ethic promises a way forward. But there is much that must be left out—or simply forgotten—in the attempt.

Amnesia

Harris asks readers to consider a situation of planet-wide memory loss and confusion. Imagine what it would be like for every person to forget everything they knew: people, facts, convictions, identities. When we all come to, we realize that we still have access to our former sources of information even though we don't know how to make sense of it all. How would we proceed? What would we consider most important for living in the world? In particular, would we turn to religion? And if so, are there any reasons to prefer the religion of Yahweh over that of Thor or Zeus?

This thought experiment is meant to reveal that most of what we cling to as having ultimate significance in life is only thought to have this status because "it was thought sacred *yesterday*."[40] I might worship God on Sundays or pray or think it is important to show reverence for a dead body, but why? Because others thought and did these things before me and I learned from them. But if there were no yesterday—if the past were erased—might we discount all religious belief equally? Beginning again from scratch, might we instead look around at our world and find more cooperative ways of living together?

Notice that Harris has provided a scenario that is a kind of original position or mythic state of nature that would be the envy of the Enlightenment. The thought that we can, or even *should*, begin again from scratch is meant to enlighten us— it would free us from the confines of the past so that we can strike out into the future with new thoughts and new solutions to our problems. If only we could imagine away the beliefs we hold for reasons such as having been taught them by others. Let us strike out on our own, dismissing all authority. *Sapere aude!* Reject tradition and the debates of the past that our forebears thought they settled.

For Harris, this is obviously not who humans are *actually*, but who we are *ideally*. And if we are ideally people who can separate ourselves from our traditions on a whim, why can't we do it now? As convalescing amnesiacs, if the untestable claims of religion would be the last thing we would attempt to recover, why do so many of us continue to believe them?

It is a revealing exercise. It champions the Enlightenment qualities of universality, individuality, and autonomy. People who are determined to think for themselves will not accept something just because a person in authority or a beloved family member also thought it. Everything must be tested according to reason. And since reason is presumably the same for everyone (one cannot simply invalidate logic because one wants to, for example), truths will be universal. Even so, it is doubtful that Harris has given us a coherent vision, let alone a compelling one. Analyzing it will allow us to get a handle on some of the shortcomings of a purportedly universal reason.

If a loved one loses her memory and struggles to relearn what is most important, none of us would—even in the minutest sense—be grateful that fate has given her a fresh start. We do not rejoice that now she can relearn only things that are strictly rational and testable, leaving behind all the clutter of her particular history. In fact, when this actually happens to people, their loved ones often experience great pain when they discover that someone they love no longer loves them in return.

As it happens, the things we consider most important are things that are *not* held by everyone else. My memories are mine and tell me who I am. As personal beings, we are beings in relations with others, so much so that we are *defined by* the relationships we have. This view of what it means to be a person is so fundamental to parts of the Christian tradition that it is used to understand God being three persons. Thomas Aquinas defined each divine person—Father, Son, and Holy

Spirit—as a "subsistent relation."[41] The personhood of each is the relationship with the other two. But they are all different, "incommunicable" relations. Who is the Father? The Father is the Father of the Son. There are no fathers without children. Who is the Son? The Son is the Son of the Father. There are no sons without fathers. Not only are the very words "Father" and "Son" relational terms, they are also how Christianity thinks about personhood. We literally know who we are as persons—and who the persons of the Trinity are—by relations with others. And who are the others? They too are persons in relations.

This theological excursus is meant to show that idealizing global amnesia is seriously misguided. According to Harris, everything you currently find important, everything that tells you that you are you, poses a grave threat to an improved world. Only by relinquishing the unique and peculiar attachments we have, and becoming generic humans from nowhere and with no history, can reason be set free to do its positive work.

I have already shown that this ahistorical view of reason has its own history. Yet it is a view that must deny its own roots in order to succeed. While it is not as though Christianity has always spoken with a single voice, it is fair to notice a significant contrast with much of what Christianity teaches about history, memory, and every other particular aspect of human existence that those in search of philosophical purity find so thoroughly offensive.

The Christian emphasis on memory is woven throughout its gospel message. When they proclaim the unlikely truth that Jesus has been raised from the dead, Christians are demonstrating a faith different from how Harris describes it. Perhaps there is an element of believing something on insufficient evidence. But like so many other matters of importance, faith here is trust. It is not so much believing *that* something is the case as trusting *in* the one who makes it so. Likewise, Christian trust is deliberately passed on in vulnerable and fragile ways. For instance, it comes by way of a female testimony of the empty tomb that would not have been legally credible in a first-century patriarchal culture. Believing their testimony is not a protest against rigorous proof. It is solidarity against those who refuse to trust vulnerable witnesses.

When Christians gather for the eucharistic feast and break bread in remembrance of Jesus's death, we both remember and in some sense reenact his suffering. We are being made into a people by what we remember together, just as we are also ennobled to live with the challenge of continually bearing the weight of the past.

Far from being something to be ashamed about, we rejoice and celebrate that we are a people of memory. Nietzsche surmised that cattle blissfully while away their time in the field chewing their cud, happy because they live without memory. But the human animal must live with the burden of remembrance, and in its collective memories, with culture. For Christians and anyone else who is learning to forgive, this means living with the wounds of the past in recognition that who I am now is partially the result of the misdeeds of others. Indeed, such are a *people* because, as persons constituted by their relations, they have been united by common memories of God's work in the world and in their midst. To be part of the Church is to declare membership with these people.

The *Catechism of the Catholic Church* has a wonderful line for use in baptisms. When the ones about to be baptized, or the godparents, are asked "What do you ask of God's Church?," the response they are to offer is "Faith!" I confess I think that's beautiful. People are not only baptized on the basis of their faith. They are also baptized in order to be in a position to receive faith from God through their brothers and sisters.

Nevertheless, if we were to picture the ideal human situation as one with no past so as to enable Harris's vision of a global community, we would be declaring a preference for knowledge that is individual rather than communal, where memory impedes pure rationality rather than serves it, and where the past only ever serves to hold us down unless we are able to consign it to utter forgetfulness. It goes without saying that then there would be no reason to learn to forgive.

*

I have concluded a chapter about the arrogance of reason by bringing up forgiveness. The reason is that forgiveness is the appropriate topic for beginning to deal with the casualties of an overly ambitious vision of the world. There is some irony in the fact that religious traditions are sometimes accused of heavy-handedness in the many ways that they have tended to wield their notions of the good life among non-believers. But there is apparently no escaping science. Some of its experts are just as prepared to tell others that they know what is best for humanity, and to endeavor to put it into practice.

In this chapter, I have disagreed with Harris concerning reason. I argued that reason not only is limited in its connection to all the complexities of our world and human existence. But more importantly, I tried to show how a failure to come to terms with the inadequacy of reason alone entails grave conceit and disguises real potential for brutality against those things labeled "unreason." I have also exposed the assumption of power that accompanies projects that purport to command a universal morality. Admitting such things need not mean extolling irrationality. Far from it. Rather, it means paying attention to what has been left out of consideration.

My point has not been simply to expose readers to the arrogance of Harris's project in hopes that they will recoil out of distaste for a conceited person. It has been that Harris is making science and reason participate in a vast program of overreach, in the course of which numerous factors are swept aside.

3

"Religion" and science

[M]oral situations are not easy to define [. . .]. It is the nature of a moral rule to be general, and its application to a particular context must be uncertain.

Mary Douglas[1]

The correct retort to the injunction "Gather ye rosebuds while ye may" is, Which rosebuds?

Alasdair MacIntyre[2]

To those outside the academic world, it may come as a surprise to learn that scholars are increasingly seeing the label "religion" as a modern invention. Far from being something obvious or given, the very idea of "religion" is constructed. The clue to grasping why it was invented and why it continues to be so pervasive in the contemporary world lies in how it is used, in what it includes and excludes. Put simply, "religion" serves to marginalize some people, movements, and cultures accused of being irrational, immoral, and violent, while protecting other people, movements, and cultures from these same allegations. In this chapter, I look at Harris's ideological use of "religion," particularly as it functions to divert attention from secular state actions. My purpose is then to show that he actually relies on Christian morality more than he realizes or cares to admit. This ideology of "religion" masks such reliance.

The ideology of "religion"

In the preceding chapters, I have for the most part simply gone along with the way that Harris and many others currently use the term "religion" in a fairly generic sense. Yet there are good reasons to insist on placing scare quotes or inverted commas around the word "religion" each time it is used (although doing so consistently is typographically tedious!). For one thing, Christians have no particular stake in claims made about "religion" in general. They have not typically accepted general observations and critiques about something called religion of the sort that Harris often makes. Growing scholarship is devoted to asking what is meant by religion. As it happens, it is not at all evident what religion means. The idea that there exist many religions of which there are many species, such as Hinduism, Christianity, and Judaism, is a modern one and has a history that is less than straightforward.[3]

For modern scholars of "religion," defining religion adequately has proven harder than one might suppose. Their search for an essential, transhistorical definition has come up empty. Some suggest that what makes a religion is a concept of a god or gods; yet there are prominent non-theistic counter-examples, such as some versions of Buddhism. Timothy Fitzgerald has argued at length that this criterion is not neutral, but is basically an extension of Christian theology.[4] Or what about the idea that religion contemplates transcendence? Here too there are significant counter-examples: why are nationalism and Marxism—with their appeals to Justice, Liberty, and History—not also considered religions? Finally, there are some who attempt to come up with *functional* definitions of religion (in which one recognizes them as religious by what they have in common *in practice*). These definitions usually focus on traits such as its absolutism, divisiveness, or irrationality. The problem is that definitions of this kind are vulnerable to secular counter-examples that display these same qualities, as William T. Cavanaugh concludes: "There is no reason to suppose that so-called secular ideologies such as nationalism, patriotism, capitalism, Marxism, and liberalism are any less prone to be absolutist, divisive, and irrational than belief in, for example, the biblical God."[5]

So how does "religion" work for Harris? I will look at several of his specific accusations, often asking how they might apply to Christianity. His main charges are that "religion" is irrational and immoral, that it is static, and that it promotes violence.

"Religion is irrational" (or immoral)

The apostles of the New Atheism are famous for their predictably ruthless attitude toward religious belief. Jacques Berlinerblau, a professor at Georgetown University, memorably asks:

> Can an atheist or agnostic commentator discuss any aspect of religion for more than 30 seconds without referring to religious people as imbeciles, extremists, mental deficients, fascists, enemies of the common good, crypto-Nazis, conjure men, irrationalists, pedophiles, bearers of false consciousness, authoritarian despots, and so forth? Is that possible?"[6]

I have already said much about this style of argument and about rationality generally. But if we needed further proof that religion is irrational, Harris notes that the "revealed religions" (Judaism, Islam, and Christianity, often also referred to as the Abrahamic faiths) make incompatible claims and therefore can't all be true. His patience is much greater with non-revealed religions such as Buddhism, which he understands to contribute "interesting" ideas about human consciousness. His ire is considerably dampened when he discusses the Dalai Lama and meditation. In fact, when asked about reincarnation at the 2006 Beyond Belief Conference, Harris said, "Who knows?"[7] As you might imagine, his otherwise sympathetic audience gasped and shouted him down: "Oh, come on!" It seems that the New Atheist charge of irrationality is not merely an attack on the *content* of specific doctrines, but on how it causes people to *behave* unreasonably. If this charge applies to Judaism, Islam, and Christianity, it has something to do with the fact that these religions can't agree with each other about the facts that are supposedly revealed. Harris's argument is that it is irrational to believe the claims of one while disbelieving the other, and disagreement leads to conflict.

The first problem is that painting this sort of picture of the three Abrahamic faiths as distinct "religions" obscures very important historical ties, collaboration, and in some cases endeavors to show the nature of their very deep theological entanglement with each other. A recent example of this entanglement is the extraordinary work of the American Lutheran theologian, Robert W. Jenson, which ties Judaism and Christianity so closely that they together present the body of Christ to the world.[8]

The second problem is that, however much it is overstated, citing incompatibility between these faiths is somewhat absurd for being so obvious. Nobody is merely "religious" in this conspicuously plain and nonspecific sense. It is hardly typical to meet a person who has tried to embrace all religions at the same time, only to be surprised and dismayed upon discovering that many of their chief tenets are at variance with each other. As it happens, people are generally followers of one religious tradition or another. (Even if we consider traditions that are blends of others, such as in Sufism and the Druze or, differently, in Sikhism, one usually speaks about a *tradition* of syncretism.) Certainly no Christian or Jew or Muslim will be awakened from her deluded religious stupor upon realizing that people of other faiths confess religious truths that their own faith denies. So what is going on here?

It is obvious and uninteresting that not all religions can be right about everything they claim. But the point Harris really wants to make is different: it is that all religions are *false*. Yet moving from "not all religions can be right" to "all religions are wrong" is no more valid as a way of reasoning than if a judge were to dismiss every case in which testimonies are in conflict. This is no mere oversight on Harris's part. It discloses his crucial assumptions about the inherently irrational nature of something called religion. Using the label "religion" already accomplishes much of the work for discrediting them—he dismisses their disagreements for being patently silly and self-refuting.

When Harris accuses religion of being immoral, he often claims that Christianity (and Islam) condone slavery and other unethical practices. What we know to be "unethical" comes from our own use of reason, further proving that religion is superfluous when it comes to moral questions. Well, only an utterly unhistorical (and, indeed, unscientific) approach to Christianity could be happy with the specifics of this argument, as can be seen on the topic of slavery.

Unfortunately many critics confuse what the Bible says about slavery with more recent colonial practices or with the kind of slavery that existed in the southern United States before the Civil War. Harris argues that nineteenth-century American abolitionists were on the right side of morality, although they used theologically indefensible arguments. When they appealed to the Bible in defense of liberating slaves, Harris accuses them of "cherry-picking" the text.[9] Elsewhere he writes, "Of course, one can cherry-pick scripture and find reasons to love one's neighbor and turn the other cheek, but the truth is, the pickings are pretty slim [. . .]."[10]

Now, it is true that the Old Testament gives clear commands about the treatment of slaves. But what is most striking is something Harris completely ignores: the Bible's trajectory of liberation that inspired the abolitionists. In the same way that Jacob sells himself into Laban's employ (Genesis 30—31) or a present-day soldier agrees to serve for a certain number of years in exchange for college funding, the slavery laws in the Bible regulate a contractual system of debt-payment for those too poor to pay by other means. It was an ancient system that, in Israel's life, provided an option for people otherwise trapped in poverty. In historical context, moreover, Israel's specific regulations regarding slavery were much more humane than its neighbors'. The regulations are oriented toward the goal of *freeing* slaves by forgiving their debts before they have been "worked off." Freedom rather than ownership is the operating principle. Harris neglects texts such as Deuteronomy 15 that call for the release of slaves every seven years. The most surprising teaching turns out to be far from Harris's simplistic claim that the Bible condones slavery; it is that the Bible requires the frequent and periodic canceling of all debts in order to eliminate poverty (Deuteronomy 15.4) and enjoins the radical redistribution of land for the same purpose (Leviticus 25).

This theme of liberation is carried into the Christian gospel in the New Testament. Jesus proclaims the release of captives and the forgiveness of debts (not just sins), declaring that the Jubilee year has come (Luke 4). One wonders whether Harris has ever heard a negro spiritual that works creatively with these themes. It is worth recalling that it wasn't scientists or atheists who succeeded in abolishing slavery in England and in the United States; it was evangelical Christians. What we see in the development of the story the Bible tells is the overturning of entrenched cultural practices of antiquity, a movement away from enslavement toward liberation. Any critic sensitive to the narrative flow of the Bible should notice this. Otherwise he is the one just cherry-picking parts of the text, lifting them from their context and ignoring other parts, for the sake of making the argument he wants to make.

"Religion is static"

The development of the Bible's story on moral questions is not just seen in the case of slavery. Through other examples, we can learn from the history of how seemingly straightforward moral commands were interpreted that it's a mistake to take all parts of the Bible at face value in the way that both fundamentalists and New Atheists do. For example, capital punishment gradually became less and less common within the history that the Bible itself recounts. Even though the death penalty is famously enjoined in the books of the Law ("an eye for an eye"), this is a way of *limiting* rather than *requiring* vengeance of this kind, an idea that encouraged practices of supplying acceptable substitutes. By the time of Jesus, the death penalty was uncommon for most offenses listed in the Old Testament.[11] If there is any doubt, Jesus specifically subverted it (John 8), and the book of Hebrews understands his death to be a sacrifice that puts an end to vengeance-killing. There are other practices commanded in the Old Testament (such as animal sacrifice) that have always been rejected by Christians. These are examples of progress and development *within* the Bible in which the interpretation of commands takes place within a larger momentum and unfolding of the Bible's own core concerns. Similarly, the whole history of Christian theology since the Bible is a history of doctrinal development.

Yet Harris cannot stomach development of this sort, whether it is within the Bible or subsequent to it. While noting that impressive developments in other fields of inquiry, notably science, are a sign of health, vitality, and accomplishment, he steadfastly assumes that all religious belief is static. He asks readers to imagine what would happen if we were to bring a fourteenth-century Christian scholar to the present day. Harris says we would be embarrassed that our time-traveler is a "total ignoramus" when it comes to scientific knowledge: his knowledge of the cosmos would be elementary; of medicine, barbaric; of dinosaurs and gene therapy, nonexistent. "But he would know more or less everything there is to know about God."[12] Why does Harris believe that Christian theology does not develop throughout time? My guess is that he is either a fundamentalist of the worst sort or else he simply knows very little about Christian theology.

It is not as though the development of all disciplines is always upward. As we have seen, the esteemed Enlightenment dream sees itself to be shining the bright light of day on every dark medieval superstition, overcoming the age of faith with the promises of unbounded progress. Development of this sort is difficult to dispute in some of the sciences: astronomy and medicine are "further along" because they work in "advances." But the picture is much more complicated if we include any subject in the humanities. Who would claim that philosophy has only improved since Socrates? Are philosophers generally wiser now than they were at the time of Aristotle? Clearly not.

The same goes for the history of Christian theology. Since Paul and the apostles, this history has neither been steadily uphill nor uniformly downhill. The trouble is that Harris acknowledges *no development at all* within it and even seems to rule it out as a possibility. He concludes that Christian belief about God (or, again, all "religious belief") is therefore illegitimate, dogmatic, and stuck in the past. He clings to the assertion that "religion, being the mere maintenance of dogma, is one area of discourse that does not admit of progress."[13] I doubt that many religious people throughout history would accept the idea that religion is merely about maintaining dogma. Harris defines religion (maintenance of dogma) so as to reach his conclusion (religion is static). Perhaps unkindly, one is tempted to ask who the real ignoramus is.

Referring to "the myth of 'moderation' in religion," Harris argues that any religious person who does not hold a frozen and dogmatically stagnant version of their faith suffers from loss of nerve in the face of countervailing cultural forces. They have given in to the pressures of modernity, perhaps. They have been quick to downplay the embarrassing or archaic aspects of their founding texts. Anyone who thinks that science and faith are not at odds, in Harris's estimation, is doing bad science and diluting their religious belief. Harris really does accept the fundamentalist description of Christianity at face value. As Jackson Lears, professor of history at Rutgers University, comments, "Belief in scriptural inerrancy is Harris's only criterion for true religious faith."[14]

In nearly all respects, Harris falls into step with fundamentalist Christianity when it comes to thinking about what a pure faith would be. He agrees with fundamentalists that genuine Christianity entails seeing science and faith as irreconcilable, rejecting modernity, and being suspicious of development. Where there are "moderate" versions of Christianity that might repulse him less, Harris discounts them as inauthentic (claiming that "religious moderation is the result of not taking scripture all that seriously"[15]). As many critics have noted, Harris appears to be able to conceive of religion only in fundamentalist terms, and so many of his arguments simply evaporate in the light of a non-fundamentalist understanding of the Bible and theology.

In his influential book, *Knowledge and Social Imagery*, David Bloor shows that there is a paradox in the history of theology and the history of science.[16] On the one hand, science and reason tend to be protected from being explained in terms of their historical, social, or political situation. They enjoy a kind of non-religious "sacredness," says Bloor. A paradox arises because when these same factors are excluded in theology and "religious" dogma generally, it is viewed as backward and superstitious.

With great irony, Bloor describes the "supernaturalism" of today's champions of reason. By requiring no further explanation of those deemed to be proceeding "rationally," while demanding quite a lot from the "irrational," today's believers in science protect science's own current dogmatic orthodoxies from questions about their social construction. By insisting that religious orthodoxy is static throughout history, Harris's dismissal of it on these grounds—however mistaken—just as surely applies to his own ahistorical account of reason itself.

Going back to the Bible, consider how Harris uses a sur-
prisingly two-dimensional set of critiques to talk about the
kind of book the Bible is thought to be. As usual, the options
are decidedly stark. "The Bible is either the word of God, or it
isn't."[17] "Either the Bible is just an ordinary book, written by
mortals, or it isn't."[18]

Harris seems to think that when they call the Bible the "word
of God," billions of Christians mean nothing more nuanced
than that "the creator of the universe wrote (or dictated) one
of our books." If God wrote it, Harris contends, we shouldn't
expect it to bear such clear and embarrassing marks of a particular people in the ancient Near East and the personalities of
individual human authors. More than this, we might expect
that the Bible would do a much better job making impressive
prophesies about the future (such as predicting the invention
of the internet). Because it doesn't do this, Harris courageously
informs Christians, "This should trouble you." He also thinks
Christians will be scandalized to discover that a description
of a round part of Solomon's palace uses only an imprecise
approximation (in cubits) of pi and that "the Bible contains no
formal discussion of mathematics." Astoundingly, Harris even
claims that the Bible couldn't have been written by the omniscient creator because it says nothing about electricity, modern
genetics, astronomy, or the cure for cancer.[19]

The point here is not only that Harris misunderstands Christian teaching about the Bible as God's word. Nor is it that he
can't really be bothered to look into it. It is that he can't fathom
that anything less than a divinely authored book dropped from
the sky (already leather bound, perhaps) might be the least bit
interesting.

The fact is that Christianity, admittedly with some modern
exceptions, doesn't fear the Bible's particular origins. Of course
it is a book written by mortals! Moreover, mortals comprised
the councils that decided which writings to include and which
to exclude. Christianity has usually been proud of how human

this whole process was, believing that God was nevertheless *with* the authors and *in* the process. Divinity and humanity are unified in similar ways throughout different domains of Christian thought. The Council of Chalcedon (AD 451) confessed Jesus to be fully God and fully human in such a way that these two are not confused or mixed; they both remain what they are, yet are united in one person. This is also a primary way of thinking about how sacraments work—God acts in human acts, yet without confusing God and humanity—in the same way that the Gospels speak about what is bound and loosed in heaven reflecting parallel earthly action (Matthew 18.18).

Similar claims of the Bible are made in Christian thought. God does not bypass the particulars of human existence in order to deliver a single, authoritative document to all time simultaneously. It is actually part of the Christian good news that God sojourns with creatures in their particular historical and cultural circumstances. This "scandal of particularity" is only a problem when theologians have hoped for a gospel of more general or universal spiritual truths. Some theology *has* gone down this road—gravely mistaken in my view—of saying that one does not need the specific history of God with the Jews and with the particular ways that theology has developed through time through conflict and negotiation. A notable example is John Hick's 1977 book, *The Myth of God Incarnate*, which assumed that because the doctrine of the incarnation was shaped by cultural factors, its validity is in doubt.[20] But orthodox Christianity has always been able to acknowledge these cultural factors, even to celebrate them. When theologians have been ashamed of the eminently human parts of the process of doctrinal development, they have been misled by a scientific view of pure progress and objectivity. In both science and theology, it was a fantasy.

The problem is not just that Harris makes mistakes about religion that would embarrass any undergraduate student. It is that his carelessness appears to be intentional since it is bound up with the ideology of "religion." He is thoroughly uninterested in what religious people actually believe and what they practice just as he leaves completely unturned the history of religious movements and traditions. He seems only interested in a pure form of "progress" that blithely and confidently dismisses the past. And so having ruled out the possibility of development within religion when it isn't clearly progress, he consigns all of the complexities of religious experience, communal worship, private devotion, and centuries of theological debate to a single dot. Given his constant proclamations about the superiority of science for its rigorous commitment to evidence, Harris is shockingly irresponsible in his investigation of religion.

"Religion promotes violence"

Among the reasons Harris believes that pointing out incompatible claims between the world's religions is an argument is his functional understanding of what constitutes "religion": incompatibility leads to conflict, especially religious violence; monotheism's insistence on a single deity is inherently intolerant and therefore dangerous.[21] It is worth dwelling on this point because quite a lot hinges on it, especially one of the standard stories told in support of secular reasoning's superiority.

The most common version of the story runs like this. In the wake of religiously divided post-Reformation Europe, wars were fought for competing religious dogmas. Unable to control the populace or to guard against allowing petty irrationalities to prevail, a new way of organizing societies—nation-states— found it necessary to intervene. These wars of religion, on the standard account, were waged until a national, rather than religious, unity was able to achieve peace. This was accomplished through fully rational and secular doctrines of governance and law, thus stilling the chaos that unchecked religious people always threaten to bring on a society.

It is very conventional to hear this story told in one form or another and Harris appears wholly to endorse it. For many, the story fits especially well with how they have come to think about religion and violence in our contemporary world, especially involving Islam. Sadly, Harris has uncritically accepted a thesis that both has recently been called into question and that serves purposes more ideologically charged than historically sound. The work of William Cavanaugh of DePaul University is required reading on this topic and, for a much fuller account, readers will want to consult Cavanaugh's writings directly.

Cavanaugh's main argument is that despite the obvious power in telling the standard story of the wars of religion, it is more of a myth than reality. The historical reality of this period is more complex than is acknowledged by the popular version. It is far from being the case that Protestants and Catholics were killing each other in the name of religious doctrine. On many occasions one finds Protestants killing Protestants and Catholics killing Catholics in the name of the newly emerging nation-state. The new, violent factor was not religious belief but *nationalism*.

It is here that the ideological character of the standard account of the "wars of religion" comes into view most clearly. Cavanaugh's careful research shows that rather than being the heroic *solution* to the violent conflicts, the nation-state was largely their *cause*. Yet with the help of the myth, religious violence is singled out in order to distract our moral attention away from secular violence. The myth's payoff is demonstrating, in Cavanaugh's words, that "Violence labeled religious is always reprehensible; violence labeled secular is often necessary and sometimes praiseworthy."[22]

We have already seen this at work in the way that Harris condemns terrorists like Osama bin Laden. Even while acknowledging that in places like his "Letter to America" bin Laden cites numerous US foreign policy matters (such as the presence of American troops in Saudi Arabia, support for the corrupt Saudi regime, and support for Israel against Palestinians),

Harris simplifies things considerably: "I will argue that we can ignore all of these things—or treat them only to place them safely on the shelf [. . .]." Instead, "We are at war with Islam."[23] Harris effectively dismisses what he might otherwise call "facts about our world"—actual political and military matters—on grounds that he has identified "religion" in the mix. Cavanaugh describes how the myth of religious violence works to Harris's advantage:

> The myth of religious violence helps to construct and marginalize a religious Other, prone to fanaticism, to contrast with the rational, peace-making, secular subject. This myth can be and is used in domestic politics to legitimate the marginalization of certain types of practices and groups labeled religious, while underwriting the nation-state's monopoly on its citizens' willingness to sacrifice and kill.[24]

In viewpoints such as Harris's, "religion" is made morally culpable for violence in our world whereas violence waged by nation-states is exempted from moral scrutiny. Cavanaugh argues that when nations wage war by stirring up nationalism within their own borders, they are relying on the successful use of what we really should call religion—if by "religion" we mean those movements and ideas for which people are most willing to give their lives, the objects of their ultimate loyalties and devotion.

Just consider how successful the secular ideological account has become. It is by now routine for critics to point out passages in the Old Testament or the Qur'an that seem to incite violence. Yet when the war-lore from one's own nation's history or patriotic music (such as "Land of Hope and Glory," "Rule, Britannia!" or the US national anthem) celebrates battle, no amount of hand-on-heart solemnity can seem to do it justice. The fact that many of these patriotic songs are also "religious" signals the way that religious violence becomes acceptable only when it serves the nation.

Particularly in nations that claim a proud heritage of secular institutions that developed in order not to privilege one religious sect over another, there has arisen a corresponding set of attitudes (ideology) that the people will largely adopt, often without knowing it. This is their tacit willingness to remove their "religious" convictions from public activities in the interest of maintaining the peace among the many diverse groups that make up the society. Religion works for the state. God gets the soul; the nation gets the body.

Morality in the meantime

When Harris discusses the limitations of science, he often focuses on its *technological* limitations rather than the limited scope of scientific investigation as such. He repeatedly expresses hope that science will converge on answers to moral questions even when it is unable to do so at the present. Even though many of our current questions cannot yet be answered in practice, the fact that they have answers *in principle* is enough to keep us committed to finding them. He gives the example of the corporal punishment of school children, asking whether it increases well-being or not (he doubts it). While it may not yet be possible to answer definitively, it is for Harris a *scientific* question and not one on which we should simply respect all views and traditions.[25]

While many people share Harris's views on the morality of corporal punishment, it is not at all clear that they do so for scientific reasons. I am more interested, though, in how Harris embodies a way of holding moral commitments that still await full vindication. Even though there are questions that cannot now be answered by science, Harris is strangely upbeat about science's ability to answer them in the future. Consider how he parts ways with famed biologist E. O. Wilson, discussed earlier.

Wilson teaches a moral program that strictly looks to evolution or to the findings of evolutionary psychology. If something is good for the survival and perpetuation of one's genes, this became codified as morality. Ethics thus originates in biology even though culture and religion subsequently find other ways of justifying and teaching it. There are clear affinities with Harris, but he departs from Wilson at a crucial point. Harris writes, "The fact that our moral intuitions probably conferred some adaptive advantage upon our ancestors does not mean that the *present* purpose of morality is successful reproduction, or that our 'belief in morality' is just a useful delusion."[26] Being moral will sometimes mean acting in *opposition* to what is given to us by evolution. If a person sacrifices the well-being of their family and friends in order to promote a stranger's well-being, they are engaging in a kind of altruism that falls outside of anything that obviously benefits their genes from an evolutionary standpoint. I think Harris is profoundly right about this. We ought to be suspicious of any morality reduced to a narrow Darwinian calculation. But it is also at this point that Harris's own preference for an alternative seems most arbitrary.

The Oxford philosopher of religion Keith Ward argues that seeking the good of all is just as rational as seeking good either for just myself or for just my friends and family. Harris's morality isn't necessarily more rational than Wilson's. As Ward says,

> It is reasonable to be a rational egoist in a world in which my pains are the only pains I am going to feel. It is reasonable to help my family and friends because I like them and am inclined to do so. And it is reasonable to aim at the general good because that is what a completely impartial agent (and reason is surely impartial) would do. All these reasons often conflict; in that case, we just have to decide what to do. [Wilson's evolution-based] sociobiology will not help, and neither will reason alone.[27]

Similarly, in a review of *The Moral Landscape* in the *New York Review of Books*, H. Allen Orr reiterates the central critique:

> Harris's view that morality concerns the maximization of well-being of conscious creatures doesn't follow from science. What

experiment or body of scientific theory yielded such a conclusion? Clearly, none. Harris's view of the good is undeniably appealing but it has nothing whatever to do with science. It is, as he later concedes, a philosophical position.[28]

Now, "undeniably appealing" is not something we should make light of. But what I want to focus on here is Harris's strikingly sanguine attitude about knowing how to negotiate the conflict between any number of (what Ward calls) reasonable alternatives. It is clear to Harris when we ought to overrule our biology in the name of morality. Moreover, even though many of science's moral findings lie in the future, we can still be fairly confident in our ability to know what is most important in the meantime.

Why should this be? I believe the answer lies in Harris's own unacknowledged background inheritance of Judeo-Christian moral conviction, especially when it comes to compassion, justice, and sacrifice. Consider the following quote: "[T]here is every reason to expect that kindness, compassion, fairness, and other classically 'good' traits will be vindicated neuroscientifically."[29] But why? Why expect this rather than the opposite? What kinds of reasons is he talking about when he says that we have "every reason" to think that science will prove these characteristics of traditional morality? If we have reasons like this now, they must be different from the *scientific* reasons that still await us. We could surely debate whether abstractions like kindness, compassion, and fairness are robust enough on their own to guide a person in their daily life (to the advice "be compassionate," one will always wonder "What is the compassionate thing to do here and now?"). Even so, I believe the point stands. If it is not science itself that has given us these insights into how we ought to live, what should we make of the sources (such as "religion") that have made them seem so obviously good while scientists work away to ratify what we already know?

The answer appears to be that science is taking the credit for what Christianity took centuries to produce so thoroughly throughout its cultures that it can now be taken for granted. Even atheism of the sort that Harris represents is believed by scholars to be the product of a particular kind of unbelief unique to Christian or post-Christian societies.[30] If so, notice how easy this makes things for Harris. Recall his arguments related to slavery. I showed before that he approaches the Bible selectively and unhistorically. But there is no need for him to be careful about using the Bible since where he wants to end up—"slavery is morally wrong"—is so easily achieved that it's absurd to think that we need the help of an ancient document. He writes,

> The moment a person recognizes that slaves are human beings like himself, enjoying the same capacity for suffering and happiness, he will understand that it is patently evil to own them [. . .]. It is remarkably easy for a person to arrive at this epiphany [. . .].[31]

To Harris, slavery is "the greatest—and the *easiest*—moral question our society has ever had to face."[32] It's important to ask why Harris is so optimistic. No arguments are needed; we only have to open our eyes to what is completely obvious—that because all people are humans, they are moral equals. Perhaps when it has not been so obvious to others, they have been blinded by religion or their own prejudice. But the real reason Harris finds the morality of slavery so uncomplicated is that he is standing on the shoulders of centuries of Western thought, including Christian and secularized Christian ideas, that make it so. Of course it is easy now; the debate is over! It is doubtful that without Jewish and Christian teaching about all humans being created in the image of God, as well as thousands of years of reflection on what this means (including quasi-secular philosophies espousing that "all men are created equal"), that our common humanity with all others on the planet would now strike Harris as obvious and "remarkably easy."

Harris identifies a number of "easy" themes that we can hold on to *in the meantime*. While humanity bides its time for science to show that compassion is something worth showing to strangers, we can trust (in what? in whom?) that we are right to show it. Harris is simply the product of a long history of moral thinking in the West that has valued things like justice and compassion, that has so internalized the virtues of the Good Samaritan and the ethic that flows from the *imago dei* that there is no sense of urgency to discover what we ought to be doing while we wait on forthcoming answers from science.

At this point, the Christian reader might expect Harris to say something the slightest bit complimentary about Christianity. But he insists that science and "religion" are antithetical and will never come to terms.[33] I confess to finding this wholly ungrateful. Given Harris's belief that someday science will vindicate the goodness of compassion and justice, one might expect him at least to acknowledge a potential point of convergence between science and religion. The best he can say about Christian morality is that when it happens to be right (as with compassion and justice, perhaps), it is coincidental. But what about the reverse? The moral concepts that science has not (yet) vindicated are ones that we hold out for because we adhere to them for a different set of unacknowledged reasons (in the case of Harris). Harris is indeed more moral than Wilson—but only because he is more Christian.

However, Harris's implicit Christian hope doesn't stop here.

The virtues of scientific knowing

Harris not only has confidence that science will vindicate particular moral commitments like one's views on corporal punishment, which may or may not *now* be held for scientific reasons. He also has a more general confidence in science's ability to answer questions of this sort. Consider: What persuades a person, such as a scientist, to stick with the agenda of a scientific morality *while it is ongoing*? Where does their future hope come from?

Notice that this is a separate question from whether science can in fact determine moral values. It points to a moral impulse that precedes science. Why would anyone choose to spend the time with science in order to find human values in the first place? It is doubtful that the answer can come from science itself. Historically, Christianity has given a theological rationale for continuing to pursue scientific questions. What is perhaps most striking about projects like Harris's is not so much the answers given to moral questions (most of his own answers are predictably traditional), but the contradictions that arise when attempting to explain why they continue to be asked.

Implied and assumed in accounts of naturalistic morality such as Harris's is a rather severe set of ethical principles about knowledge. By "severe" I mean *exacting* and even *formidable*. In order for the project of a "science of morality" to get off the ground, those who engage in it must possess a whole host of convictions: attentiveness, critical thinking, a dogged pursuit of truth, and a patient commitment to discovering it no matter where it is to be found. One must also approach the world with the conviction that it is intelligible to begin with, that reason works rather than fails us. There is a fearlessness that ideally lies at the heart of scientific pursuits. Researchers strive for an objectivity that is willing to accept the truth about our world no matter what it turns out to be. Even if they happen to be disquieting or go against accepted opinion, the sheer facts about the way things are ought to determine the outcome of the research. Roman Catholic theologian John Haught writes,

> The naturalistic ethic is demanding, almost puritanical in its moral rigor: the responsible knower is one who becomes detached from pre-scientific ways of seeing and understanding. Right knowing requires not just cognitive growth but also a painful process of moral development.[34]

It takes a great deal of moral development to strive for the kind of objectivity that science values (leaving aside the question of whether such objectivity is about to be achieved in practice). In fact, however fashionable it is at present to blame the Church for obstructing scientific process, it was on theological grounds that the moral virtues of scientific investigation most flourished. For example, we must believe in the value of truth (this is a moral commitment) in order to continue to use reason, especially when its results are not what we wanted. While it is true that Christians have not always and everywhere exhibited a dogged dedication to uncovering the truth of reality no matter where it is found, this is a commitment that belongs to Christian thought.

As a result, all academic disciplines were able to specialize and focus on their own work because of an underlying confidence in the unity of all truth. Things ultimately cohere in the mind of God. Why devote time to investigating anything? The traditional answer that made Western science possible had to do with these theological convictions about the ultimate coherence of all there is. Yet because "all there is" is too complex to study all at once or by the same methods, it was appropriate for there to be a variety of separate sciences to devote themselves to the study of different parts of the universe, yet always in recognition of the whole.

The university is a creation of Christianity and the oldest universities—Bologna, Cologne, Paris—were associated with the Church and linked to monasteries. Less widely known is that the diversity of subjects flowered according to a theological rationale. Convinced that the whole universe belongs to God, researchers could feel at ease about pursuing non-theological topics without worrying that they had left God behind. This confidence in God's governance over all things led in time to the highly specialized diversity of subjects, generating a model reflected by modern universities. These commitments were not the product of science, but are the same Christian legacy that produced modern science itself. Scientific investigation was free to excel in its own manner, fostering the appropriate virtues along the way.

It goes without saying, however, that quite a lot of contemporary science sees no need for theological assumptions of this sort. But what has not disappeared is the confidence these assumptions bequeathed to science, which, in some cases, has been transformed into the most disagreeable kind of hubris. The point here is not to lament the loss of theology's influence. It is to acknowledge that when science is touted as the sole fount of moral thinking, such pronouncements are *already* the result of moral commitments with a definite history. And they are commitments and values that were not the spontaneous products of scientific investigation; they were products of Christianity.

Deeper questions remain: Why pursue the truth at all? Why value reason rather than unreason? Why value facts about the world? Why not rather believe fantasies? Of course many of us *do* believe fantasies. But I suspect Harris is right when he says that our minds do not seem wired to accept without distress or even insanity beliefs that we *know* to be fantasies. We must have a "feeling for the truth" in order to use reason.[35]

Yet in asking why we should pursue the truth and devote ourselves to reason at all, Harris seems content to answer that we simply do; it is in the nature of the brain to do so. But is it so simple? If dogged pursuit of the truth were simply a fact about how things are, this still doesn't tell us that we ought to value facts about how things are. As Terry Eagleton observes, "If we are to defend reason, we must be inspired by more than reason to do so."[36] To admit as much is not to send us spiraling into unreason or superstition. It is a way of being honest that there are more factors at work than reason itself.

Friedrich Nietzsche, the nineteenth-century German philosopher not known for his friendliness to Christianity, was troubled by this very question. He noticed that we are strongly motivated by the *will to truth*, the desire to know what is the case. Even though not everything we know or believe is true, the will to truth is still at work. Any time a critique is made, it is the will to truth in action. What troubled Nietzsche most is that the will to truth seems to defy investigation. Or, more accurately, to investigate it is already to begin too late, since it is the *reason* for investigating anything at all. If one inquires after it, wonders what it is—why it is so important to us—the inquiry is itself the answer.

> [Y]ou will have gathered what I am getting at, namely, that it is still a *metaphysical faith* upon which our faith in science rests—that even we knowers of today, we godless anti-metaphysicians, still take *our* fire, too, from the flame lit by the thousand-year-old faith, the Christian faith which was also Plato's faith, that God is truth; that truth is divine.[37]

Like Harris, Nietzsche wanted to be committed to a purely naturalistic ("anti-metaphysical") account of the world. He reserved his most severe criticisms for versions of Christianity that distract believers from the world, their eyes directed only heavenward (although he mistakenly assumed that *all* versions of Christianity do this). But when he turned his attention to what he calls faith in science, he discovered that he only ran into paradoxes. The will to truth cannot be denied because it will actually be employed in the course of denying it, hence actually affirming it. It is just there as a kind of given.

Notice that this is a different conclusion from Harris's. Where Harris is content to say that our brains simply will the truth, Nietzsche is more philosophical: we seem to desire the truth because of something intrinsic and, at some level, unavoidable about the truth itself. I will not claim that this is a proof of God. Indeed, Nietzsche suspected that the will to truth masks a deeper, often malicious, compulsion toward control and mastery. But it complicates Harris's picture in more ways than he acknowledges, and over which Nietzsche's own less dogmatic atheism genuinely puzzled—in my view, to his considerable credit.

Conclusion

In 2006, Sam Harris appeared on the American political comedy program, *The Colbert Report*. When asked by the puzzled host, Stephen Colbert, why he is an atheist, Harris responded, "We're all atheists with respect to Poseidon. Anyone worshiping Poseidon, even at sea, is a lunatic." It was a clever response. But Colbert's response to Harris was, to my mind, even cleverer. Colbert replied that the issue is not that a Poseidon-worshipper is *crazy*, but that he is *wrong*.[38]

It's hard to know how seriously Colbert meant his remarks. But I understood him to be saying that the reason no one worships many of the gods of old has nothing to do with becoming so scientific and rational that no one has need of them. It is rather that Christianity (mostly) defeated them theologically and culturally. Reason itself could now flourish *within* a Christian ethos. In light of Christian theology and practice, the pagan gods no longer had a place *as gods*. As Terry Eagleton puts it, the Christian God does not exist alongside creation as though God plus the universe makes two.[39] Compared to this God who transcends all things, the gods of old were demoted and put in their place within the universe. This was a triumph of Christianity, not a triumph of science and reason on their own.

This exchange between Harris and Colbert exhibits the core of this chapter's argument: that there are many ways that science is parasitic on "religion." With this chapter, I have been particularly interested to show how "religion" can function ideologically in the hands of those who want to divert attention from either (1) an unfounded confidence in certain untested moral values or even in scientific research itself, or

(2) political projects that underwrite nation-state violence as being rational, thereby condemning all other violence as irrational and so justly making those who wage it into victims of secular aggression.

The final chapter looks at how Christian morality surpasses Harris's account.

4

A better (but strange) landscape

———•◦•———

Christian morality is a thing *so* strange that it must be declared immoral or amoral according to all other human norms and codes of morality.

John Milbank[1]

In the church, moral commands tell what we may reasonably do because Christ is risen, which otherwise could be thought irresponsible.

Robert W. Jenson[2]

Up to this point, I have critiqued Sam Harris's work in various ways. I have accused him of feigning objectivity and universality while he actually advances an ethic of and for the powerful. I have also shown that his key claims are either philosophically dubious or join up with largely discredited elements of Enlightenment philosophy. Even though I affirm his positions on many concrete moral issues, his overall vision of the moral landscape is flawed at best and despotic at worst.

Even so, no one should be content with these critiques on their own. No matter how strong or clever they may be, they won't amount to much unless one can provide a more fitting and persuasive account in its place. In this final chapter, I need to show that Christianity offers a better landscape. I believe that Christian thinkers can do better than Harris in two ways: in addressing the shortcomings of a science of morality and in the attractiveness of its own moral vision.

Better? Perhaps I should really say *strange*. The epigraph above is from John Milbank, who is *defending* Christian morality by calling it strange. There are good reasons to think that the best descriptions of morality surpass anything we would come up with on our own if we set our minds to it. This may mean straying into areas that Harris would no doubt call unreasonable, possibly even immoral—and certainly strange. But strange *is* better. I'll explain.

*

In this chapter, my strategy is to present a Christian moral vision rooted in the story of Jesus. I argue three interrelated points using Christianity's most decisive language: incarnation, crucifixion, and resurrection. With *incarnation*, I argue that following the way of Christ restores the original and proper functioning of our full humanity. God became human, embodying the good news to humanity rather than simply declaring it. So living the moral life that the good news makes possible requires much more of us than the weighing of moral facts. We are *formed* rather than *informed*. Harris's program, in contrast, is primarily limited to the accumulation of facts and information provided by science. Next, the event at the heart of Christianity—the *crucifixion*—flies in the face of judgments about human well-being. It neither celebrates death nor avoids it at all costs. It shows that a good, moral life might not be effective for much. It can even appear counter-productive and self-defeating. But these are central to any act of self-giving love that sacrifices well-being even when there is no guarantee of a good outcome. Harris's understanding of well-being is too limited to inspire anything this extreme. Finally, the *resurrection* of Jesus points to a new, redeemed humanity that lies beyond every calculation of cause and effect. It is an impossible and undreamt of life, rising again from death in vindication or consummation of everything that is true, good, and just. The vision for the good that lies beyond death isn't simply "heaven" (opposed to earth). It is a way of living with oneself and others that refuses to be restricted to what is straightforwardly accomplished in the usual ways or what presents itself on a horizon within our grasp. Harris looks to the horizon for a morality that is often commendable. But he cannot see beyond it.

Incarnation – beyond knowledge

Christian teaching about the incarnation of Christ is deeply relevant to the question about what makes us moral. The idea with the incarnation is not just that the Son of God became human. Nor is it that in becoming human, he simply taught esoteric religious concepts. But Christ shows us a fully human life. Rather than imagining that our humanity is something to overcome or to work against (as some philosophers have thought), Christianity teaches that becoming Christlike *increases* our humanity. In this way, morality has more to do with formation than information, more to do with who we become rather than what we know. It is more about the character of individuals and communities than the accumulation of relevant facts for determining the most moral course of action.

The twentieth-century Dominican theologian Herbert McCabe (1926–2001) wrote eloquently about Christ being the most human of all of us. We are to take our cues for what constitutes a fully human life from the kind of person Jesus Christ is and how he lived. McCabe explains that moral theologians following Thomas Aquinas have discussed how the virtues are involved in enhancing our humanity:

> Virtue, whatever else it means, at least means being more human; it would not be virtuous if it did not. Sin, whatever else it means, means being less human, more still, cold, proud, selfish, mean, cruel, and all the rest of it.[3]

Our humanity is less than it should be. We are less patient and more guarded, less caring and more self-centered, less loving and more estranged from each other than is humanly good for us. Our problem is not that we are material and long to be released from the weight of bodies. Nor is it that we are creatures and long to be gods. The problem is that we are sinners. Sin is something that is lost—the space opened up by the loss itself—rather than something with positive existence on its own. "We should help people to become more fully human," writes South African Archbishop Desmond Tutu. "Become what you are."[4] More fully human is what Christ is. The human rebellion against God is also a departure from our true nature. So what can be done? How do we learn to be more human?

Some things are more or less straightforward to learn. You learn the countries' capitals by memorizing them, by setting your mind toward categorizing the relevant facts. And while quite a lot falls into this kind of model, Christianity has followed an older tradition of Greek reflection on the nature of the moral life by insisting that how we learn it goes much deeper. It goes far beyond the accumulation of information and more closely resembles formation.

In particular, a great deal of Christian reflection has been devoted to expanding on the goal of Christian ethics understood as the formation of character and the ability to make prudent judgments. Confronted with a situation in which one was not specifically trained, the moral person will show sound judgment in negotiating the unknown. There is no specific and particular way to prepare for it; there are only the habits and dispositions that the tradition calls the virtues. If I visit a foreign country, I will try to learn what I can ahead of time. But what will serve me the best is if I can work toward being a "seasoned traveler." I can try to become someone who, quite apart from the specific knowledge of a place, can take the unfamiliar in his stride, with patience, grace, and poise.

When thought of this way, the goal of morality lies beyond knowledge, properly speaking. Rather, it issues in action. While it may yield concepts, ideas, and principles, these are merely steps along the way rather than the end itself. Christian morality may help us conceive what moral existence looks like and, for example, how to make faithful decisions. But even this will include a picture of the life of faith that the Christian person will actually come more closely to resemble the more she grasps it. It's only because there exists such a thing as competency and skill in living a particular way that it's possible for anyone to reflect on Christian morality as a knowledge or discipline in the traditional sense. Notice that this differs significantly from what Harris thinks—that morality is basically knowledge.

Just imagine what it would take to learn to juggle. Even though there are books on how to do it, reading them will only get you so far. The reason is that juggling is a *skill*. You would never claim to "know" juggling if all that you could do was give instructions to others about it. Your knowing juggling would be, quite simply, how we would talk about the fact that you could juggle! In fact, it's impossible to imagine anyone writing *How to Juggle* if there didn't exist people who have mastered the skill. There would literally be nothing to write about if the expertise didn't first exist.

So among the most important things to consider when it comes to gaining the skills of moral living are things like discipline, training, and practice. *All* of these are conspicuously absent from Harris's projects, and this recalls one of its most significant shortcomings, something I have addressed from a number of angles: even if science gives us the *information* we need to maximize well-being, a great deal of moral *formation* is required to decide that it is worth acting on. There's much more to moral questions than what we know. I may know that I ought to help a beggar or some other stranger in need. I might reason that doing so will increase her well-being, possibly even mine. I may also reason that if we all helped strangers in need, the world would be a better place, therefore we all ought to do it (this is Immanuel Kant's famous "categorical imperative").

Missing, though, will be the things that touch me most deeply. Do I feel compassion for another human being? Will my love compel me to a level of service that might put my own well-being at risk? The idea that we must aim higher than merely *acting* morally is dear to the Christian tradition. St. Anselm prayed, "Lord, make me taste by love what I taste by knowledge; let me know by love what I know by understanding."[5] He might also have prayed that in addition to being kind to strangers, he would feel compassion and have tenderness of heart toward them.

Why is this kind of formation important? Why be concerned with becoming a generous and compassionate person rather than simply obeying reason when it says to help a stranger? Because it is more human to be compassionate rather than to police our empathy. Short of this, acting morally—according to what science and reason tell us to do—may involve working *against* our desires. A person may be troubled by her conscience and her moral knowledge—what she knows she ought to do—even though she does not feel compassion. The only measure of "morality" in this case would be whether or not the person helps out the stranger. This is Harris's project. The moral person is sometimes moved to act in *opposition* to her desires.[6] For this view, ethics is a matter of restraint and discipline, of careful management, restriction, and keeping things in check.

Perhaps either way the stranger receives the aid she needs. The point is not that acting out of compassion rather than obeying reason will always lead to a better outcome. It is that the compassionate person acts in concert with her emotions and desires—as a whole human person. With the development of character, you will less frequently experience a crisis of conscience. Instead, you will approach a serene compatibility between desire and act as both are conformed to what is good. The moral life, in short, will truly be doing what you want to do.

Consider the life of Jean Donovan (1953–1980). She was a lay Catholic missionary to El Salvador who ran a food program for refugees of that country's brutal civil war. Along with three American nuns, Donovan was raped and murdered by Salvadoran security forces. Two weeks before her death, she wrote in a letter,

> Several times I have decided to leave El Salvador. I almost could except for the children, the poor bruised victims of this insanity. Who would care for them? Whose heart could be so staunch as to favor the reasonable thing in a sea of their tears and loneliness? Not mine, dear friend, not mine.[7]

The life and death of Jean Donovan is a witness to the incarnation. She embodied the moral extremity of compassion at great risk to her own well-being. She *wanted* to serve the children in El Salvador and wasn't compelled by a sense of guilt or obligation. Tempted by the "reasonable thing," she cast it aside to do the compassionate thing. Reason would have sent her home; compassion kept her with the Salvadoran children. It is striking to recall Harris's picture of the "good life" that I described in Chapter 2. It is a happily married, dual-income couple with "wealth and connections" who receive a billion-dollar grant to fund their charity. It is a life of reason that costs them nothing. Donovan's was a life of compassion that cost her everything. Compassion picks up where reason ends. Some will call her decision to stay the height of irrationality, foolishness, and irresponsibility. But they will say this only because the "reasonable thing" has set their sights too low on a morality that is merely knowledge. Donovan chose the better life.

Crucifixion – beyond calculation

Harris is not wholly mistaken to link morality with how our actions promote well-being. But morality is more than this. At a basic level, the Christian morality I've been describing is good for our humanity regardless of how it addresses problems in the world. It does not need some evil to oppose, some lives to save, or some innocents to protect. Goodness is a deeper reality than evil and does not simply react against it.

Having said this, Christianity also expects that what is good for those who live moral lives will also bring about benefits for others. In Luke's Gospel, Jesus begins his ministry declaring that he will bring "good news to the poor." Christians have long noted that following what Jesus taught would enact a radical redistribution of wealth that will directly benefit those caught in poverty. As I mentioned in the last chapter, ancient Israel was to have no permanent underclass. Israel was commanded to perform a periodic and ongoing canceling of debts, a return to ancestral lands that had been sold off due to some misfortune, and a release of debt-slaves (see Leviticus 25). Related to this is the larger vision of the Sabbath over which Jesus frequently sparred with religious leaders (e.g. Matthew 12, Mark 3). What is good news for the poor was not categorically good for everyone. It was bad for the rich in particular. They failed to see how their participation in the acts of God might be a joyful sharing in divine goodness, glory, and plenty. The rich man goes away sad because he hears the good news as bad news (Mark 10.22).

So my point is not that Christian morality has nothing to do with well-being, but that it is more than this. What is good cannot be judged by looking *exclusively* at the effects of actions. Why not?

For one thing, it's unclear how long we should wait to begin assessing the effects of our actions. I may do something that only years later makes sense of the good others will want to attribute to it. Some things may not bear fruit, as it were, until the people responsible for them are long gone. A person may waste their most productive years caring for a diseased child who might not have existed if a different decision had been made prior to birth. What should we think in the meantime? It is not as though moral judgments on these actions are unconnected from effects. It is just that the business of judging something to be good is more complicated than Harris allows.

Related to this, there are actions that, no matter the time-scale, quite simply seem to benefit no one. Yet sometimes we want to say that even if someone is too weak to have much of an effect on anyone's well-being, they still did the right thing. It is significant that the story of Jesus holds up a victim of injustice and sovereign power as a model to follow. By taking the victim's perspective, Christianity is able to see what has been left out or sacrificed by moral schemes designed by and for the power-ful. Those who have power will use their ability to accomplish things to measure what is good. But there is both a powerless-ness and a pointlessness to Jesus's cross. It is not clear that it will benefit anybody. The cross is not a wager that something posi-tive will happen if Jesus remains committed to his movement unto death. Yet for Christians this is the consummate moral act. Jesus isn't just at the mercy of other people who are in the position to weigh moral decisions. He is himself a moral actor.

It's true that Christians will point to the timescale in which Jesus's resurrection validates the goodness of his obedience unto death. The crucifixion need not be remembered merely as an ineffectual and tragic failure. But the good news about God raising Jesus from the dead is a message for the rest of humanity, for those whose deaths still await resurrection. This difficulty is experienced as Holy Saturday, the unbearable gap between cross and resurrection that is only traversed by hope. There are no calculations to perform, no research that will show beyond doubt that crosses produce resurrections.

Living between cross and resurrection means that there is a crucial disconnect between ethical living and the good, real-world effects that may otherwise be cited as its justification. Loving your enemies may or may not convince enemies that there is a better way. At times, acting on behalf of justice may improve lives including your own. Other times it will get you killed and the injustice will remain. Talk of martyrdom always makes Harris nervous because he immediately thinks of suicide bombers. But the Christian celebration of its martyrs is very different. We remember them for their peaceable witness to Christ and their refusal to compromise when it became apparent that the tide of public opinion was not going to go in their favor.

How are Christian martyrs able to refuse to compromise? For one thing, they aren't driven by short-term results. This would make martyrdom quite impossible. Instead, identifying one's death with the death of Christ radically qualifies all talk of effects, outcomes, and benefits. And this disconnect between faithfulness and its benefits is good news. It is too crass to reduce it simply to a hope for heaven. It is belief that what is true, just, and good will prevail despite the forces of falsehood, injustice, and evil. In the words of a sixteenth-century Anabaptist theologian, "Truth is unkillable." Christian martyrs can die joyfully, even blessing their killers, because they trust that their deaths share in the death of Christ. And if God could raise him from the dead, God can raise the martyrs too.

An example will help make this point. In 2005, Tom Fox, an American Christian aid worker from Virginia, was in Baghdad working with Iraqi families who were trying to locate missing loved ones. He was abducted and held hostage along with three others by a group called the Swords of Righteousness Brigade. The group issued their demands to the US government. Several months later, Fox's body was found wrapped in plastic and dumped in a street in Baghdad. He had been tortured and shot to death. Tom Fox had considered the risk but didn't allow preoccupation with short-term results to hold him back. Fox was a Quaker and held their beliefs about nonviolence and pacifism. Here are some words from his blog:

> It seems easier somehow to confront anger within my heart than it is to confront fear. But if Jesus and Gandhi are right then I am not to give in to either. I am to stand firm against the kidnapper as I am to stand firm against the soldier. Does that mean I walk into a raging battle to confront the soldiers? Does that mean I walk the streets of Baghdad with a sign saying "American for the Taking"? No to both counts. But if Jesus and Gandhi are right, then I am asked to risk my life and if I lose it—to be as forgiving as they were when murdered by the forces of Satan. I struggle to stand firm but I'm willing to keep working at it.[8]

Fox's determination to follow in the way of Jesus meant struggling to be able to be forgiving in the face of killers. I find it fascinating that this is what he means by standing firm. The day before he was abducted, Fox wrote an article called "Why Are We Here?"

> We are here to root out all aspects of dehumanization that exist within us. We are here to stand with those being dehumanized by oppressors and stand firm against that dehumanization. We are here to stop people, including ourselves, from dehumanizing any of God's children, no matter how much they dehumanize their own souls.[9]

The dehumanization that Fox and his friends were committed to stopping was not only evident in the victims of violence. It is also present in the tendency we all have to hold ourselves back from forgiving the violent ones. For Fox, working against dehumanization meant restoring the full humanity of others through the process of becoming more human himself. Before going to one of the most dangerous regions of the world, Fox had signed a "statement of conviction" in case he was hurt or killed. The statement reads:

"We reject violence to punish anyone. We ask that there be no retaliation on relatives or property. We forgive those who consider us their enemies."[10]

I tell the story of Tom Fox because I think we need to admit just how *strange* it is. Preemptive forgiveness! This is no straightforward humanitarianism. It's not particularly rational or measured. It may or may not increase the aggregate well-being in the world. There's no thought that Fox's killers will be moved by this extraordinary act of compassion or that Baghdad would become less violent as a result.

Yet Tom Fox is a witness to the cross of Jesus. Fox's life and death expose the limited nature of appeals to responsibility, utility, and calculation. Relieved of making morality ensure that things come out right, the Christian is set free for loving enemies, forgiving them, and for joy. Joy in particular is keyed to this non-instrumentality. When you do something for the joy of doing it, you may also have other reasons for it. But the joy is likely to trump them all. And if you imagine an activity—like dancing, perhaps—that you do simply for the sheer pleasure of doing it, you have a sense of how closely joy really is keyed to non-instrumentality.

It's no coincidence that loving falls into this category of things we do for their own sake. We don't love for a *reason*. When it's true and genuine, love doesn't ask what can be gained by it or what it can achieve. It finds joy in its sheer exercise. But not all loving is manifestly and obviously for the joy of it. In fact, unrequited love is notoriously the stuff of tragedy and despair. Love is exercised as movement in its back-and-forth quality. It's given for the joy of it in a giving that exposes you to the possibility that it will go unmet. Love is a desire that, in a sense, can only be understood by the logic of love itself. You can't appreciate what love is all about simply through definitions or descriptions. You can gather as much information about love as you want to, but if you have been deprived of love all your life, this information will not do much. In fact, to ask the question "Why love?" is already to make clear that you misunderstand what love is all about.

The things most worth doing are done for their own sakes and not for what they bring about. In this sense, Christian morality is very similar to loving. The joy of living a Christian life exceeds all talk of demands, outcomes, obligations, and duties. A lot of moral philosophy has been occupied with each of these things. But the overflowing, spontaneous, and unbounded nature of Christian goodness exposes just how limited the alternatives are. If the will to love and forgive regardless of the consequences—and even positively in the face of overwhelming tragedy and vulnerability for doing so— is itself love's most perfect flourishing, then the more one's will to the good is transformed out of love for God, the more morality truly comes into its own. But this is not the same as offering a reason or justification for loving. Instead, we are pushed toward loving without limits. Christian moral existence contradicts our tendency to hold ourselves back from making ourselves full gifts to others.

That said, Jesus and Tom Fox were killed on account of living this way. So even though a more fully human life may be keyed to joy, it is a joy that is far from straightforward.

Resurrection – beyond reason

The Christian moral life might not be the key to well-being in anything like the uncomplicated sense that Harris means it. Recall the New Atheist message displayed on London buses, "There's probably no God. Now stop worrying and enjoy your life." The implication that God is the only thing standing in the way of an enjoyable life says something about how simplistically and narrowly the New Atheists understand life—it sounds to me like "Just go about your daily shopping in comfort." (Notice also how meaningless this message is for the young woman in Harris's vision of the "bad life" who flees from child soldiers. I discussed this in Chapter 2.)

By contrast, what Christians call good may ruin your life, lose you your friends, estrange you from family members, frustrate your career path, and lead to a premature death. Nevertheless, none of these things is at odds with joy and happiness. As it happens, we're generally poor judges of well-being, goodness, and happiness. The reason is a limited imagination—we can only envisage a world no more complex than what we can manage. The resurrection of Jesus radically expands what is possible.

Here's a personal story that illustrates what I mean. Years ago I was walking in downtown Los Angeles with a friend named Greg. A man came up behind us, cursing and trying to provoke us into a confrontation. Puzzled and scared, especially since we hadn't done anything to deserve this, I walked on, hoping that the man would give up and walk away. But Greg turned and held out his hand in greeting, saying, "My name's Greg. What's yours?" The man didn't shake hands, but promptly turned and left. I was astounded. In those short moments, I had been preparing for something completely different. What had just happened? Perhaps the man couldn't stand being treated like a person. Or maybe hearing Greg's name disarmed him since now his opponent was an individual with an identity. All I know is that Greg and I had been invited to respond to this situation with anger and aggression, qualities that would no doubt have been met in return. But Greg was wiser than I was. And the risk he took changed the dynamics of the whole encounter.

In this story, I represent morality as we usually think about it. We're presented with situations and have difficult decisions to make. Faced with a violent threat? Prepare to fight to defend yourself and your loved ones. Sometimes and much more commonly, we are already making decisions without even knowing it. What is common to every case, though, is that we interpret what is presented to us as givens. We see ourselves responding to a very limited set of options. We are fundamentally convinced that things are basically what they appear to be and we can only work with what we have.

Expand the threatening scenario from the streets of LA to tensions between nations and the usual convictions still apply. Nothing could be more reasonable than taking a "realist" approach to war, as Harris does. On this view, the reality of violence and injustice makes it unrealistic to cling to ideals about nonviolence. In fact, refusing to fight is positively unconscionable. For Harris, the "false choice of pacifism" is "flagrantly immoral."[11] Because we're always tempted to assume that the givens are all we have to work with, our imaginations are too small. But Christian morality is stranger than this. In the story, Greg represents the strangeness of Christian morality because he somehow imagined a state of affairs beyond the givens. A whole different world is possible.

The philosopher of religion Mary-Jane Rubenstein, of Wesleyan University, argues that this is the crucial difference between Christian morality and Harris's. She claims that, at its best, Christianity envisions possibilities beyond what appear to be a hopelessly bleak array of limited options. She quotes from Daniel Berrigan, the renowned Catholic peace activist. In a recent keynote address called "Study War No More," Berrigan reflected on the prophet Isaiah's ridiculous promise: "They shall beat their swords into plowshares" (Isaiah 2.4). He asked, "Didn't Isaiah know you can't beat a sword into a plowshare?" Doesn't Isaiah know how irresponsible it would be to stop studying war? Clearly it's ridiculous.

> Isaiah announces the impossible. I call it the necessary impossible. The absolutely crucial impossible, the impossible that must come to pass. He summons what shall come to pass precisely because it is impossible. "They shall beat their swords into plowshares." A terrifying experiment. The crucial must somehow be joined to the improbable. Something new, something beyond all effort and imagining, must come to be. Swords into plowshares. The image is crucial to the prospering of any culture, to the survival of

individuals, to honor, to religious faith, to a civilized sense of one another, crucial, finally, to the faith of the earth. But, but, but. The oracle is also impossible. Who then—who now—believes it could come to pass? After Vietnam, Grenada, Panama, Nicaragua, El Salvador, Afghanistan, Iraq—who still believes? Therefore the conclusion of Isaiah. Because the task is necessary and because it's radically impossible, therefore, it must be done. [. . .] The worst time, Isaiah dares imply, is the apt time. It's the time when our hands drop in helplessness and resources fail. This is the time of the toppling of those thrones, if only we believed. [12]

Belief in resurrection means believing that the impossible, irresponsible, ridiculous tasks may still be done. This is the meaning of faith. Faith isn't believing things without sufficient evidence, but having a vision that risks refusing to accept the choices we've been asked to make within the terms provided, the definitions given, and the explanations offered. As Rubenstein says, it is "a vision of an impossible world order, where torture and war and inequality are always unacceptable." Without faith that things might be (impossibly) better than we can reasonably hope, we are content to settle for what is possible and call it moral.

This is also what it means to speak of transcendence. Rightly understood, Christianity's notion of transcendence doesn't whisk believers out of the everyday. It presses them more firmly into it. It doesn't promise deliverance from the difficulty of living in a compromising world. Nor does it soothe consciences that remain there, determined to make the most of things. Instead, it's a transcendence that sees beyond the present impasses toward possibilities that aren't presently on the table. Yes they are *impossible* possibilities. They're impossible because they aren't thought of, they don't compute, and they don't make sense according to the rules we're working with. It's true that this aspect of Christianity has sometimes been misunderstood, poorly exercised, and outright spurned. But these departures should be recognized for what they are:

genuine failures to let Christian faith inspire the determination to look beyond what appear to be dead ends by seeing another way.

A heroic insistence on taking the world only as it presents itself to us is what argues for the superiority of reason, science, and fact. But these are all limited in a very important sense. It is not simply that there are ways of knowing that exceed them, as though by "faith" religious people are simply admitting that they have bungled purer forms of questioning. It is rather that faith begins where reason ends. Faith thinks when thinking cannot. Søren Kierkegaard called this the ultimate paradox of thought: "to want to discover something that thought itself cannot think."[13] We cannot think our way to the unthinkable any more than we can reason ourselves into the absurd. Nietzsche was right, "There is always some madness in love. But there is also always some reason in madness."[14]

I hope it's evident that there's a "beyond" to reason that's not simply *unreason*. When Christianity conceives of well-being and happiness, it stretches the boundaries of what is possible because it knows resurrection. So these concepts (happiness and well-being, to which we should add goodness) are by no means straightforward. It's true that happiness is a concept that Christian moral theologians have traditionally reached for in order to explain a more fully human life. But it hasn't tried to deny the profound disruption and disorientation that such a life produces and may even require when is it most authentically human. The more seriously deformed the setting (politically, socially), the greater the cost a moral existence is likely to exact. But as Berrigan says, "the worst time is the apt time." This is nothing new to a Church skilled in remembering those who have suffered for the faith. So what are we to make of happiness? Only that it must refer to the kind of well-being or contentment that, despite everything else, is able to look back over a life of faith and obedience and call it good. The fact that others may have to do this for me once I am gone merely demonstrates how the Church, rather than the individual, is the setting for this looking back.

Furthermore, as I said above, the disconnect between moral living and its effects doesn't lie in goodness somehow being at odds with our human nature. It's rather a function of the fact that the world we have made for ourselves is a crucifying world.[15] The forces of dehumanization have no patience for those who live more fully human. By contrast, the seeming prosperity of the wicked—a question so poignant in the Psalms and in Job—has nothing to do with anything intrinsic about wickedness. The world is so thoroughly disordered that it is actually aligned with wicked actions and designs. The Bible is not only concerned with the fact that, as humans, we are sinners. It also shows that sinners are perfectly at home in a sinful world, with structures, institutions, and modes of exchange that run on sin and even positively reward it. Dissonance and disruption are thus normal for those who refuse to live by them.

Most sobering of all is that even arguments such as I've laid out (like that the joy of Christian existence is its release from being instrumentalized for some purpose) are bound to undo themselves if Christian morality really is more about living than arguing, loving rather than knowing, and making disciples rather than having debates. We'll never be able to say anything more true than the claims our living make.

This is why I'm not really trying to prove anything here. I have serious reservations about the kind of Christian apologetics that tries to prove that it's right. In this mode, arguments threaten to take the place of living in truth and so will surely refute themselves in exact proportion to their success. The more they win, the more they concede. The more convincing a proof-apologist is, the less convincing the Church needs to be through its existence as a people formed by the gospel. And by "convincing," perhaps we really should say "strange"—and that's not always very convincing!

This making-strange activity is what Christians mean by witness. The temptation to direct the query about goodness on to something other than the life of the Church is nothing other than the hope to evade the necessity of ourselves embodying the gospel's truth. Put starkly, if Christians can't point to Christianity's goodness, they should refrain from claiming that, despite all appearances to the contrary, it really is quite true. Because it seriously affects Christian claims about goodness, the sex-abuse scandal currently plaguing the Roman Catholic Church really does threaten the truth of the gospel. When Christianity's critics keep bringing up topics like this, they are cutting much deeper than they know. We either need to stake the gospel's truth on its goodness or not at all.

This is why Christianity must always be able to produce people like Jean Donovan and Tom Fox. Witnesses wouldn't dare to point to the truth of something without also showing lives that flow from that conviction. All of their arguments are secondary to this. The American theologian Jonathan Tran says this doesn't mean arguments have no place. Arguments, Tran claims, "help us make sense of martyrdom, namely, why in the world someone would die for God. In the absence of disciples who die for God, we offer arguments."[16]

In other words, morality may very well be part of the problem if it conceives of itself primarily as a knowledge, since it will invariably draw us away from life and discourage us from being more human rather than less. Nietzsche worried that this is what philosophy does, and precisely (he thought) because it's too Christian. It tempts us away from the rough ground of living and toward a purer and more abstract form of existence than we actually have. The answer to these tensions is not a people armed with the truth. It is a people whose goodness lies partly in their determination not to allow the truth they proclaim to outpace their single-minded devotion to its display in their common life. The language Christians have usually adopted for this is *church*, just as its native language for this display is *joy*.

Conclusion

As I've said before, I don't imagine that any of this will necessarily convince anybody. It would be perfectly rational to dismiss it. It's true that Jean Donovan and Tom Fox don't *prove* that Christianity is true (although I wouldn't believe it if it never produced lives like theirs). But they do give a sense of what's so utterly strange about Christian morality. From practices like preemptive forgiveness to loving one's enemies to blessing one's killers; from subordinating the immediate outcomes of our actions to trusting the final triumph of truth and goodness; from happiness and joy that are less than obvious to conceiving of our full humanity as both natural and constantly eluding us—none of these is where reason alone is likely to take us. Ironically perhaps, it also strikes me that the Christian refusal to make calculations about happiness and well-being actually attests to a profound respect for true happiness and genuine well-being themselves. Their fulness is beyond strict calculation. At stake is what it means to be human and to know a good and happy life.

So . . . What makes us moral? The answer is not one we would have come up with on our own, even with the assistance of scientists. For morality is not something we can create simply by our own efforts. We would not have guessed that loving enemies is anything but perverse, confused, and even suicidal. To us it's strange, and far from what we would tend to think of as good news. But if we (not to mention our enemies!) find we need it more than we think we do, it might just lift us above our limited horizons—beyond what seems sensible based on quantifying costs and benefits or weighing pros and cons.

Anything less may certainly be moral, reasonable, and responsible in some sense. But it is a limited sense. For the followers of Christ, the mysteries of incarnation, cross and resurrection mean that more, much more, is possible.

Notes

Preface

1 John Howard Yoder, *Body Politics: Five Practices of the Christian Community Before the Watching World* (Scottdale, Penn.: Herald, 1992), 69.

Introduction

1 Cited in Alister McGrath, *The Twilight of Atheism* (New York: Doubleday, 2004), 78.

2 Sam Harris, "Is Religion 'Built Upon Lies'?," *Beliefnet*, January 17, 2007, <http://www.beliefnet.com/Faiths/Secular-Philosophies/Is-Religion-Built-Upon-Lies.aspx?p=2>.

3 The term was coined by Gary Wolf in "The Church of the Non-Believers," *Wired* 14.11 (November 2006):1.

4 Friedrich Nietzsche, "On the Uses and Disadvantages of History for Life," in *Untimely Meditations*, trans. R. J. Hollingdale (Cambridge: Cambridge University Press, 2004), sec. 1.

5 Friedrich Nietzsche, *Thus Spoke Zarathustra*, in *The Portable Nietzsche*, ed. and trans. Walter Kaufmann (London: Viking Penguin, 1968), part 1, sec. 2.

6 For this formulation I am indebted to Mary-Jane Rubenstein, "A Faith in Ends: Sam Harris and the Gospel of Neo-Atheism" (presented at a meeting of the Wesleyan Alumni Association, Durham, North Carolina, June 3, 2007).

7 Sam Harris, *The Moral Landscape: How Science Can Determine Moral Values* (London: Free Press, 2010), 177.

8 Michael O. Emerson and Christian Smith, *Divided By Faith: Evangelical Religion and the Problem of Race in America* (Oxford: Oxford University Press, 2000), esp. 8–9.

9 Kwame Anthony Appiah, "Science Knows Best," *New York Times*, October 1, 2010, <www.nytimes.com/2010/10/03/books/review/Appiah-t.html>.

10 Terry Eagleton, *Reason, Faith, and Revolution: Reflections on the*

God Debate (New Haven: Yale University Press, 2009), 37.

11 Ludwig Wittgenstein, *Culture and Value*, trans. Peter Winch (Chicago: University of Chicago Press, 1984), 56e.

1 The gospel according to Sam Harris

1 Sam Harris, *The Moral Landscape: How Science Can Determine Moral Values* (London: Free Press, 2010), 202 n. 17.

2 There are a few serious problems with how Harris uses "religion." I discuss these in Chapter 3.

3 Sam Harris, "Science Must Destroy Religion," *Edge: The World Question Center*, 2006, <http://www.edge.org/q2006/q06_7.html#harriss>.

4 Harris, *Moral Landscape*, 24.

5 Harris, "Science Must Destroy Religion."

6 Christine J. Walley, "Searching for 'Voices': Feminism, Anthropology, and the Global Debates over Female Genital Operations," *Cultural Anthropology* 12.3 (1997): 405–38 (406–7).

7 Walley, "Searching for 'Voices'," 409.

8 Stephen Toulmin, *Cosmopolis: The Hidden Agenda of Modernity* (Chicago: University of Chicago Press, 1990).

9 Sam Harris, "A Response to Critics," *Huffington Post*, January 29, 2011, <http://huffingtonpost.com/sam-harris/a-response-to-critics_b_815742.html>.

10 Harris, *Moral Landscape*, 133–4.

11 Sam Harris, "A Response to Critics."

12 "Terry Eagleton – The New Atheism" (n.d.), video clip, YouTube, <http://www.youtube.com/watch?v=codtM-WnS3w>.

13 For example, see Sam Harris, *The End of Faith: Religion, Terror, and the Future of Reason* (London: W. W. Norton & Company, 2004), 53: "We will continue to spill blood in what is, at bottom, a war of ideas."

14 Harris, *End of Faith*, 199.

15 Harris, *End of Faith*, 199.

16 Harris, *End of Faith*, 203.

17 Sam Harris, "Why I'd Rather Not Speak About Torture," *Sam Harris The Blog*, April 28, 2011, <http://www.samharris.org/blog/item/why-id-rather-not-speak-about-torture1>.

18 Harris, *End of Faith*, 198.

19 Harris, *Moral Landscape*, 61–2.

20 Harris, *Moral Landscape*, 31.

21 Harris, "Why I'd Rather Not Speak About Torture."

22 Harris, *Moral Landscape*, 181.

23 Harris, *Moral Landscape*, 95–6.

24 Thomas Nagel, "The Facts Fetish," *The New Republic* (October 20, 2010): 30–31, emphasis added.

25 While Harris praises scientists who speak with nuance and caution about subjects in their own field (*Moral Landscape*, 124), all bets appear to be off when weighing in on religion.

26 Sam Harris, "In Defense of Profiling," *Sam Harris The Blog*, April 28, 2012, <http://www.samharris.org/blog/item/in-defense-of-profiling>.

27 <http://muslimswearingthings.tumblr.com/>.

28 Harris, *End of Faith*, 29.

29 "Sam Harris and Scott Atran Discussion (2 of 3) – Beyond Belief 2006," (n.d.), video clip, YouTube, <http://www.youtube.com/watch?v=Wu6qQDphSGU>.

30 Talal Asad, *On Suicide Bombing* (New York: Columbia University Press, 2007), 46–7.

31 Robert Pape, *Dying to Win: The Strategic Logic of Suicide Terrorism* (New York: Random House, 2005), 4.

32 Asad, *Suicide Bombing*, 45.

33 When asked by *TED Talks*' Chris Anderson about women who chose to wear a burqa out of mistrust of male lust or other reasons, Harris expressed suspicion of the reasons given: "We have to be honest about the constraints that these women are placed under. And so I think we shouldn't be so eager to always take their word for it, especially when it's 120 degrees out and you're wearing a full burqa." Sam Harris, "Science Can Answer Moral Questions," *TED Talks*, Feb. 2010, <http://www.ted.com/talks/sam_harris_science_can_show_what_s_right.html>.

34 Slavoj Žižek, "Liberalism as Politics for a Race of Devils," *ABC Religion and Ethics*, Nov. 22, 2011, <http://www.abc.net.au/religion/articles/2011/11/22/3373316.htm>.

35 Alister McGrath, *Why God Won't Go Away: Is the New Atheism Running on Empty?* (Nashville: Thomas Nelson, 2010), 104.

36 Žižek, "Liberalism as Politics."

37 H. Allen Orr, "The Science of Right and Wrong," *The New York Review of Books*, May 12, 2011, <http://www.nybooks.com/articles/archives/2011/may/12/science-right-and-wrong/>.

38 These quotes come from Sam Harris, *Letter to a Christian*

Nation (New York: Alfred A. Knopf, 2006), 66–7, 3, 5, 50 and 5 respectively.

39 E.g. Ludo de Witte, *The Assassination of Lumumba*, trans. Renée Fenby and Ann Wright (New York: Verso, 2001).

40 E.g. Robert W. Green, *Protestantism and Capitalism: The Weber Thesis and Its Critiques* (Boston: D. C. Heath and Company, 1959).

41 See David Bentley Hart, *Atheist Delusions: The Christian Revolution and its Fashionable Enemies* (New Haven: Yale University Press, 2009), Ch. 4.

42 Cf. G. C. Peden, *British Rearmament and the Treasury, 1932–1939* (Edinburgh: Scottish Academic, 1979) and Robert Boyce, *The Great Interwar Crisis and the Collapse of Globalization* (New York: Palgrave Macmillan, 2009).

43 Harris, *Letter to a Christian Nation*, 67.

44 Harris, *Moral Landscape*, 158.

45 William H. Swatos, Jr., "The Relevance of Religion: Iceland and Secularization Theory," *Journal for the Scientific Study of Religion* 23.1 (1984): 32–43 (39).

46 N. J. Demerath III, "The Rise of 'Cultural Religion' in European Christianity: Learning from Poland, Northern Ireland, and Sweden," *Social Compass* 47.1 (2000): 127–39. Swatos describes Iceland in similar terms to Sweden: very tolerant in religious matters but hardly pluralistic (Swatos, "Relevance of Religion," 36).

47 Harris, *Letter to a Christian Nation*, 40.

48 Antony Flew, *Thinking About Thinking* (London: Fontana, 1989).

49 James Wood, "The Celestial Teapot," *The New Republic*, December 18, 2006, <http://www.tnr.com/article/the-celestial-teapot>.

50 Fritz Redlich, *Hitler: Diagnosis of a Destructive Prophet* (Oxford: Oxford University Press, 1998).

51 Harris, *Letter to a Christian Nation*, 43.

52 Harris, *Letter to a Christian Nation*, 33.

53 Suppose there are two communities of excellent scientists, the only difference is that one seeks, through their science, the well-being of conscious creatures while the other seeks its opposite. We might decide to call them good and evil. But what is the message of the good community to the bad one? Isn't it simply, "Use your science for global well-being!"? But if so, then they

will hardly be drawing on their scientific knowledge in doing so.
54 Paul Virilio, *The Original Accident* (Cambridge: Polity, 2007).

2 The arrogance of reason

1 Sam Harris, *The Moral Landscape: How Science Can Determine Moral Values* (London: Free Press, 2010), 124.
2 Sam Harris, *Letter to a Christian Nation* (New York: Alfred A. Knopf, 2006), 75.
3 Mary Douglas, *Purity and Danger: An Analysis of Concepts of Pollution and Taboo* (Harmondsworth, Middlesex: Penguin, 1970), 52. Douglas cites E. E. Evans-Pritchard, *Nuer Religion* (Oxford: Oxford University Press, 1956), 84. See also Stanley Hauerwas, *The Peaceable Kingdom: A Primer in Christian Ethics* (Notre Dame: University of Notre Dame Press, 1983), 116–17.
4 Sam Harris, "Science Can Answer Moral Questions," *TED Talks*, Feb. 2010, <http://www.ted.com/talks/sam_harris_science_can_show_what_s_right.html>.
5 Richard Dawkins, *A Devil's Chaplain: Reflections on Hope, Lies, Science, and Love* (New York: Mariner, 2004), 34.
6 E. O. Wilson, *Consilience* (London: Little, Brown, 1998), 280.
7 Jeffrey Stout, *Democracy and Tradition* (Princeton: Princeton University Press, 2003), 266–9.
8 Russell Blackford, "Book Review: Sam Harris's *The Moral Landscape*," *Journal of Evolution and Technology* 21.2 (December 2010): 53–62, <http://jetpress.org/v21/blackford3.htm>.
9 Peter Singer, "The Great Debate" (presented at Arizona State University, November 6, 2010), video clip, YouTube, <http://www.youtube.com/watch?v=3wCNJJwIPY4>.
10 Blackford, "Book Review."
11 Harris, *Moral Landscape*, 11.
12 Sam Harris, "Response to Critics," *Huffington Post*, January 29, 2011, <http://www.huffingtonpost.com/sam-harris/a-response-to-critics_b_815742.html>.
13 Harris, "Response to Critics."
14 Harris, *Moral Landscape*, 15.
15 Harris, *Moral Landscape*, 69.
16 Harris, *Moral Landscape*, 69.
17 I acknowledge that I am making these scenarios do more work than Harris intended. But I think they are fair game since he admits that his entire thesis about science being able to

determine morality turns on whether we can distinguish clearly and absolutely between well-being in these two images.

18 Harris, *Moral Landscape*, 16.

19 United Nations Security Council, *Final Report of the Panel of Experts on the Illegal Exploitation of Natural Resources and Other Forms of Wealth of the Democratic Republic of Congo* (New York: United Nations Security Council, 2003). I am grateful for the work of John Kiess on these topics.

20 D. M. Tull, *The Reconfiguration of Political Order in Africa: A Case Study of North Kivu (DR Congo)* (Hamburg: Institut für Afrika-Kunde, 2005), 167–78.

21 Harris, *Moral Landscape*, 71.

22 Most recently, Harris has developed what he considers to be a critique of free will. He maintains that free will is an illusion since our thoughts and actions can be detected on the neuro-logical level moments before we have conscious thoughts about them. Harris's approach to the problem of will seems to be to deny it, a conception that he believes should influence our crim-inal justice systems: criminals should be rehabilitated rather than punished since, in some sense, they could not have done otherwise. While this strikes me as a simplistic approach to a complex issue, I notice Harris's consistent gravitation toward the language of determinism, just as the subtitle of *The Moral Land-scape* declares that science can "determine" moral values. Har-ris's response to Augustine, therefore, might simply be to point to something in our brains in order to understand a weak will. But if so, I see nothing in his program that attempts to address how our wills might be repaired, apart from his nightmarish scenario discussed in the previous chapter, in which those with degenerate desires are given a "firmware update." This ought to serve as a warning about just what is involved in science "deter-mining" moral values. If we understand this in the strong sense, as I think we should, then Harris's denial of free will ought to be seen as a way of making room for his vision of the thought police.

23 Harris, *Moral Landscape*, 63, emphasis original.

24 Harris, *Moral Landscape*, 171.

25 Harris, *Letter to a Christian Nation*, 30.

26 Harris, *Letter to a Christian Nation*, 31.

27 Harris, *Moral Landscape*, 171.

28 Harris, *Letter to a Christian Nation*, 29–30.

29 Sam Harris, "A New Science of Morality," *The Edge*, September 17, 2010,<http://edge.org/conversation/a-new-science-of-morality-part-3>.

30 Virginia Moreira and Nelson Coelho Junior, "The Phenomenology of Schizophrenic Experience: A Cross-Cultural Critical Study Brazil-Chile," *Terapia Psicológica* 21.2 (2003): 75–86.

31 Jonah Lehrer, "The Truth Wears Off: Is There Something Wrong With the Scientific Method?" *New Yorker*, December 13, 2010, 1–6.

32 Tara Parker-Pope, "Cancer Funding: Does It Add Up?" *Well: Blog of the New York Times*, March 6, 2008, <http://well.blogs. nytimes.com/2008/03/06/cancer-funding-does-it-add-up/>.

33 Jonathan LaPook, "The Disparity in Cancer Research Funding," *CBS Evening News*, May 27, 2009, <http://www.cbsnews. com/2100-18563_162-5044528.html>.

34 Alister McGrath, *Why God Won't Go Away: Is the New Atheism Running on Empty?* (Nashville: Thomas Nelson, 2010), 11. McGrath cites <http://www.publishersweekly.com/pwprint/ 20061120/15976-bestsellers-from-the-academy-.html>.

35 Lehrer, "The Truth Wears Off."

36 Harris, *Moral Landscape*, 20.

37 Robert A. Nisbet, *The Quest for Community: A Study in the Ethics of Order and Freedom* (New York: Oxford University Press, 1953), 6. Of Bentham, J. S. Mill wrote, "There is hardly anything in Bentham's philosophy which is not true. The bad part of his writings is his resolute denial of all that he does not see, of all truths but those which he recognizes" (*Dissertations*, i. 356).

38 Immanuel Kant, "An Answer to the Question: 'What is Enlightenment?'," in *Kant: Political Writings*, ed. Hans Reiss, trans. H. B. Nisbet (Cambridge: Cambridge University Press, 1970).

39 For example, see David Bloor, *Knowledge and Social Imagery*, 2nd edn (Chicago: University of Chicago Press, 1991).

40 Sam Harris, *The End of Faith: Religion, Terror, and the Future of Reason* (London: W. W. Norton & Company, 2004), 24.

41 Thomas Aquinas, *Summa Theologica*, I, Q. 29, a. 4.

3 "Religion" and science

1 Mary Douglas, *Purity and Danger: An Analysis of Concepts of Pollution and Taboo* (Harmondsworth, Middlesex: Penguin, 1970), 155.

2 Alasdair MacIntyre, *A Short History of Ethics* (New York: Touchstone, 1966), 32.

3 Paul J. Griffiths, "The Very Idea of Religion," *First Things* (May 2000); Pankaj Mishra, "How the British Invented Hinduism," *New Statesman*, August 26, 2002.

4 Timothy Fitzgerald, *The Ideology of Religious Studies* (Oxford: Oxford University Press, 2000).

5 William T. Cavanaugh, *The Myth of Religious Violence: Secular Ideology and the Roots of Modern Conflict* (Oxford: Oxford University Press, 2009), 55.

6 Jacques Berlinerblau, "Secularism: Boring (Part I)," *Washington Post*, July 16, 2007, <http://newsweek.washingtonpost.com/onfaith/georgetown/2007/07/secularism_boring_part_i.html>.

7 "Sam Harris and Scott Atran Discussion (3 of 3) – Beyond Belief 2006," (n.d.), video clip, YouTube, <http://www.youtube.com/watch?v=BRKbBsl6KaQ>.

8 Robert W. Jenson, "Toward a Christian Theology of Judaism," in *Jews and Christians: People of God*, ed. Carl E. Braaten and Robert W. Jenson (Grand Rapids: Eerdmans, 2003).

9 Sam Harris, *Letter to a Christian Nation* (New York: Alfred A. Knopf, 2006), 17–18.

10 Sam Harris, "Is Religion 'Built Upon Lies'?," *Beliefnet*, January 17, 2007, <http://www.beliefnet.com/Faiths/Secular-Philosophies/Is-Religion-Built-Upon-Lies.aspx?p=2>.

11 Glen Stassen, "Biblical Teaching on Capital Punishment," in *Capital Punishment: A Reader,* ed. Glen Stassen (Cleveland: The Pilgrim Press, 1998); John Howard Yoder, *The Christian and Capital Punishment* (Newton, Kan.: Faith and Life, 1961).

12 Sam Harris, *The End of Faith: Religion, Terror, and the Future of Reason* (London: W. W. Norton & Company, 2004), 22.

13 Harris, *End of Faith*, 22.

14 Jackson Lears, "Same Old New Atheism: On Sam Harris," *The Nation*, April 27, 2011, <http://www.thenation.com/article/160236/same-old-new-atheism-sam-harris>.

15 Harris, "Is Religion 'Built Upon Lies'?"

16 David Bloor, *Knowledge and Social Imagery*, 2nd edn (Chicago: University of Chicago Press, 1991), esp. 183–5.
17 Harris, *Letter to a Christian Nation*, 3.
18 Harris, *Letter to a Christian Nation*, 5.
19 References in this paragraph are to Harris, *Letter to a Christian Nation*, 79, 60–1.
20 John Hick, ed., *The Myth of God Incarnate* (Philadelphia: Westminster, 1977).
21 This claim about the danger of monotheism is extremely common. For an example, see Harris, *End of Faith*, 93.
22 Cavanaugh, *Myth of Religious Violence*, 121.
23 Harris, *End of Faith*, 109. See "Full text: bin Laden's 'Letter to America,'" *The Observer*, November 24, 2002, <http://www.guardian.co.uk/world/2002/nov/24/theobserver>.
24 Cavanaugh, *Myth of Religious Violence*, 4.
25 Sam Harris, *The Moral Landscape: How Science Can Determine Moral Values* (London: Free Press, 2010), 4.
26 Harris, *Moral Landscape*, 48.
27 Keith Ward, *The Big Questions in Science and Religion* (Conshohocken, Pa.: Templeton Foundation Press, 2008), 205.
28 H. Allen Orr, "The Science of Right and Wrong," *New York Review of Books*, May 12, 2011, <http://www.nybooks.com/articles/archives/2011/may/12/science-right-and-wrong/>.
29 Harris, *Moral Landscape*, 80.
30 E.g. Stephen Bullivant, "Atheism, Apologetics and Ecclesiology: *Gaudium et Spes* and Contemporary Unbelief," in *Imaginative Apologetics: Theology, Philosophy and the Catholic Tradition*, ed. Andrew Davison (London: SCM Press, 2010), 90.
31 Harris, *Letter to a Christian Nation*, 18–19.
32 Harris, *Letter to a Christian Nation*, 18, emphasis original.
33 Harris, *Moral Landscape*, 10.
34 John F. Haught, *Is Nature Enough?: Meaning and Truth in the Age of Science* (Cambridge: Cambridge University Press, 2006), 151.
35 Harris, *Moral Landscape*, 126.
36 Terry Eagleton, *Reason, Faith, and Revolution: Reflections on the God Debate* (London: Yale University Press, 2009), 128.
37 Friedrich Nietzsche, *The Gay Science*, trans. Josefine Nauckhoff (Cambridge: Cambridge University Press, 2004), sec. 344.
38 "The Colbert Report," Comedy Central, April 25, 2006, <http://

www.colbertnation.com/the-colbert-report-videos/62694/
april-25-2006/sam-harris>.
39 Eagleton, *Reason, Faith, and Revolution*, 6–7.

4 A better (but strange) landscape

1 John Milbank, *The Word Made Strange: Theology, Language, Culture* (Oxford: Blackwell, 1997), 219.
2 Robert W. Jenson, *Systematic Theology: The Works of God* (Oxford: Oxford University Press, 1999), 2:209, emphasis added.
3 Herbert McCabe, *God Still Matters* (London: Continuum, 2002), 96.
4 Desmond Tutu, "Becoming More Fully Human," in *Voices from the Heart: A Compassionate Call for Responsibility*, ed. Eddie and Debbie Shapiro (New York: Jeremy P. Tarcher / Putnam, 1998), 277.
5 *The Prayers and Meditations of St. Anselm*, trans. Benedicta Ward (New York: Penguin, 1973), 237.
6 In this respect, Harris appears to be in agreement with Kant, who wrote that "the will is a faculty of choosing only that which reason, *independently of inclination*, recognizes as practically necessary, i.e., as good." Immanuel Kant, *Foundations of the Metaphysics of Morals*, in *Critique of Practical Reason and Other Writings in Moral Philosophy*, trans. Lewis White Beck (Chicago: University of Chicago Press, 1949), 72, emphasis added.
7 Ana Carrigan, *Salvador Witness: The Life and Calling of Jean Donovan* (Maryknoll, NY: Orbis Books, 1984), 218.
8 Tom Fox, "Fight or Flight?," *Waiting in the Light Blog*, October 22, 2004, <http://waitinginthelight.blogspot.com/2004/10/fight-or-flight.html>.
9 Tom Fox, "Why Are We Here?," *Peace*, Jan–Mar 2006, 26, <http://peacemagazine.org/archive/v22n1p26.htm>.
10 "We Mourn the Loss of Tom Fox," *Peace and Justice Support Network of the Mennonite Church USA*, March 10, 2006, <http://peace.mennolink.org/articles/tomfox.html>.
11 Sam Harris, *The End of Faith: Religion, Terror, and the Future of Reason* (London: W. W. Norton & Company, 2004), 199.
12 Mary-Jane Rubenstein, "A Faith in Ends: Sam Harris and the Gospel of Neo-Atheism" (presented at a meeting of the Wesleyan Alumni Association, Durham, North Carolina, June 3, 2007).
13 Søren Kierkegaard, *Philosophical Fragments*, ed. and trans.

Howard V. Hong and Edna H. Hong (Princeton: Princeton University Press, 1985), 37. I owe this point to Rubenstein.

14 Friedrich Nietzsche, *Thus Spoke Zarathustra* (1883–85), in *The Portable Nietzsche*, ed. and trans. Walter Kaufmann (London: Viking Penguin, 1968), 153. See also Plato's *Phaedrus*, in which Socrates attests that there are many forms of madness praised by the *wise* but not the *learned*.

15 Herbert McCabe, *Law, Love, and Language* (London: Continuum, 2003), 132.

16 Jonathan Tran, unpublished paper on Christian analytic philosophy of religion.

Further reading

———— •••• ————

Key works by Sam Harris

The End of Faith: Religion, Terror, and the Future of Reason. London: W. W. Norton & Company, 2004.

"In Defense of Profiling." Sam Harris The Blog, April 28, 2012. <http://www.samharris.org/blog/item/in-defense-of-profiling>.

"Is Religion 'Built Upon Lies'?" Beliefnet, January 17, 2007. <http://www.beliefnet.com/Faiths/Secular-Philosophies/Is-Religion-Built-Upon-Lies.aspx?p=2>.

Letter to a Christian Nation. New York: Alfred A. Knopf, 2006.

The Moral Landscape: How Science Can Determine Moral Values. London: Free Press, 2010.

"A New Science of Morality." The Edge. September 17, 2010. <http://edge.org/conversation/a-new-science-of-morality-part-3>.

"A Response to Critics." Huffington Post, January 29, 2011. <http://www.huffingtonpost.com/sam-harris/a-response-to-critics_b_815742.html>.

"Sam Harris and Scott Atran Discussion (3 of 3) – Beyond Belief 2006," n.d., video clip, YouTube. <http://www.youtube.com/watch?v=BRKbBsl6KaQ>.

"Science Can Answer Moral Questions." TED Talks, February 2010. <http://www.ted.com/talks/sam_harris_science_can_show_what_s_right.html>.

"Science Must Destroy Religion." Edge: The World Question Center, 2006. <http://www.edge.org/q2006/q06_7.html#harriss>.

"Why I'd Rather Not Speak about Torture." Sam Harris The Blog, April 28, 2011. <http://www.samharris.org/blog/item/why-id-rather-not-speak-about-torture1>.

Other classic New Atheist texts

Dawkins, Richard. The God Delusion. London: Bantam, 2006.

Dennett, Daniel C. Breaking the Spell: Religion as a Natural Phenomenon. New York: Viking Penguin, 2006.

Hitchens, Christopher. *God Is Not Great: How Religion Poisons Everything*. New York: Twelve, 2007.

About Sam Harris or the New Atheism

Appiah, Kwame Anthony. "Science Knows Best." *New York Times*, October 1, 2010. <www.nytimes.com/2010/10/03/books/review/Appiah-t.html>.

Armstrong, Karen. *The Case for God*. New York: Alfred A. Knopf, 2009.

Berlinerblau, Jacques. "Secularism: Boring (Part I)." *Washington Post*, July 16, 2007. <http://newsweek.washingtonpost.com/onfaith/georgetown/2007/07/secularism_boring_part_i.html>.

Blackford, Russell. "Book Review: Sam Harris's *The Moral Landscape*." *Journal of Evolution and Technology* 21.2 (December 2010): 53–62. <http://jetpress.org/v21/blackford3.htm>.

Davison, Andrew, ed. *Imaginative Apologetics: Theology, Philosophy and the Catholic Tradition*. London: SCM Press, 2010.

Eagleton, Terry. *Reason, Faith, and Revolution: Reflections on the God Debate*. New Haven: Yale University Press, 2009.

Hart, David Bentley. *Atheist Delusions: The Christian Revolution and Its Fashionable Enemies*. New Haven: Yale University Press, 2009.

Haught, John F. *God and the New Atheism: A Critical Response to Dawkins, Harris, and Hitchens*. Louisville, Ky.: Westminster John Knox Press, 2008.

Lears, Jackson. "Same Old New Atheism: On Sam Harris." *The Nation*, April 27, 2011. <http://www.thenation.com/article/160236/same-old-new-atheism-sam-harris>.

McGrath, Alister. *The Twilight of Atheism*. New York: Doubleday, 2004.

McGrath, Alister. *Why God Won't Go Away: Is the New Atheism Running on Empty?* Nashville: Thomas Nelson, 2010.

Markham, Ian S. *Against Atheism: Why Dawkins, Hitchens, and Harris are Fundamentally Wrong*. Oxford: Blackwell, 2010.

Nagel, Thomas. "The Facts Fetish." *The New Republic* (October 20, 2010): 30–33.

Orr, H. Allen. "The Science of Right and Wrong." *The New York Review of Books*, May 12, 2011. <http://www.nybooks.com/articles/archives/2011/may/12/science-right-and-wrong/>.

Rubenstein, Mary-Jane. "A Faith in Ends: Sam Harris and the Gospel of Neo-Atheism." Presentation at a meeting of the Wesleyan

Alumni Association, Durham, North Carolina, June 3, 2007.

Wolf, Gary. "The Church of the Non-Believers." *Wired* 14.11 (November 2006).

Wood, James. "The Celestial Teapot." *The New Republic* (December 18, 2006). <http:// www.tnr.com/article/the-celestial-teapot>.

About science and reason

Bloor, David. *Knowledge and Social Imagery*, 2nd edn. Chicago: University of Chicago Press, 1991.

Haught, John F. *Is Nature Enough?: Meaning and Truth in the Age of Science*. Cambridge: Cambridge University Press, 2006.

Lehrer, Jonah. "The Truth Wears Off: Is There Something Wrong with the Scientific Method?" *New Yorker*, December 13, 2010, 1–6.

Ward, Keith. *The Big Questions in Science and Religion*. Conshohocken, Pa.: Templeton Foundation Press, 2008.

Wilson, E. O. *Consilience*. London: Little, Brown, 1998.

Žižek, Slavoj. "Liberalism as Politics for a Race of Devils," *ABC Religion and Ethics*, Nov. 22, 2011. <http://www.abc.net.au/religion/articles/2011/11/22/3373316.htm>.

About "religion"

Asad, Talal. *On Suicide Bombing*. New York: Columbia University Press, 2007.

Cavanaugh, William T. *The Myth of Religious Violence: Secular Ideology and the Roots of Modern Conflict*. Oxford: Oxford University Press, 2009.

Demerath III, N. J. "The Rise of 'Cultural Religion' in European Christianity: Learning from Poland, Northern Ireland, and Sweden." *Social Compass* 47.1 (2000): 127–39.

Fitzgerald, Timothy. *The Ideology of Religious Studies*. Oxford: Oxford University Press, 2000.

Griffiths, Paul J. "The Very Idea of Religion." *First Things* (May 2000).

Mishra, Pankaj. "How the British Invented Hinduism." *New Statesman* (August 26, 2002).

Pape, Robert. *Dying to Win: The Strategic Logic of Suicide Terrorism*. New York: Random House, 2005.

Swatos, Jr., William H. "The Relevance of Religion: Iceland and Secularization Theory." *Journal for the Scientific Study of Religion* 23.1 (1984): 32–43.

Other Christian sources

McCabe, Herbert. *God Still Matters.* London: Continuum, 2002.

McCabe, Herbert. *Law, Love, and Language.* London: Continuum, 2003.

Radcliffe OP, Timothy. *What Is the Point of Being a Christian?* London: Burns & Oates, 2005.

Stassen, Glen. "Biblical Teaching on Capital Punishment." In *Capital Punishment: A Reader.* Edited by Glen Stassen. Cleveland: Pilgrim, 1998.

Yoder, John Howard. *Body Politics: Five Practices of the Christian Community before the Watching World.* Scottdale, Penn.: Herald, 1992.

Yoder, John Howard. *The Christian and Capital Punishment.* Newton, Kan.: Faith and Life, 1961.

Philosophical sources

Buckley, Michael J. *At the Origins of Modern Atheism.* New Haven: Yale University Press, 1987.

Kant, Immanuel. *Foundations of the Metaphysics of Morals.* In *Critique of Practical Reason and Other Writings in Moral Philosophy.* Translated by Lewis White Beck. Chicago: University of Chicago Press, 1949.

Kierkegaard, Søren. *Philosophical Fragments.* Edited and translated by Howard V. Hong and Edna H. Hong. Princeton: Princeton University Press, 1985.

MacIntyre, Alasdair. *A Short History of Ethics.* New York: Touchstone, 1966.

Nietzsche, Friedrich. *The Gay Science.* Translated by Josefine Nauckhoff. Cambridge: Cambridge University Press, 2004.

Nietzsche, Friedrich. "On the Uses and Disadvantages of History for Life." In *Untimely Meditations.* Translated by R. J. Hollingdale. Cambridge: Cambridge University Press, 2004.

Nietzsche, Friedrich. *Thus Spoke Zarathustra.* In *The Portable Nietzsche.* Edited and translated by Walter Kaufmann. London: Viking Penguin, 1968.

Toulmin, Stephen. *Cosmopolis: The Hidden Agenda of Modernity.* Chicago: University of Chicago Press, 1990.

Virilio, Paul. *The Original Accident.* Cambridge: Polity, 2007.

Index

Index

Index

Index

truth xi, 8, 21, 49, 100–1; pursuit of
    76–9, 91; unity of 77; *see also* will
    to truth
Tutu, D. 85

universal morality xvi, 2, 20, 47,
    49–51, 56
university (as a creation of
    Christianity) 77
utilitarianism 51

Virilio, P. 26
virtues 75, 77–8, 84–5

Walley, C. 4–5
war 10, 45, 70, 96–7; in Congo 36–8;
    see also Just War

"war on terror" 9
Ward, K. 72–3
"wars of religion" 68–9
well-being principle 1, 7, 13, 25–6,
    28–9, 30–3, 36–8, 40–3, 45–7,
    71–2, 83, 86–90, 94–5, 98, 101,
    106 n. 53, 108 n. 17
will 40–2, 94, 112 n. 6; to truth 79;
    see also free will
Wilson, E. O. 30–1, 71–2, 75
witness 55, 100
Wittgenstein, L. xviii
Wood, J. 25

Yoder, J. H. ix

Žižek, S. 18–19

122